The Story of David

After God's Heart

Ian Coffey

D1350125

Authentic

SPRING HARVEST

Equipping the Church for action

First Published in 2003 and reprinted in 2004 and 2005 by
Spring Harvest Publishing Division and Authentic Media

11 10 09 08 07 06 05   9 8 7 6 5 4 3

Authentic Media
9 Holdom Avenue, Bletchley, Milton Keynes, MK1 1QR, UK
and 129 Mobilization Drive, Waynesboro, GA 30830-4575, USA
www.authenticmedia.co.uk

British Library Cataloguing in Publication Data

A catalogue record for this book is available from
the British Library

ISBN 1-85078-485-X

Cover design by fourninezero design.
Print Management by Adare Carwin
Printed in Great Britain by Haynes, Sparkford, Yeovil, Somerset

For Chris, Steve, Jon and Ali
May you continue to grow as men after God's heart

Contents

Contents

Acknowledgements

Different people have played a part in the preparation of this book and I record my gratitude to them all.

To the church family at Mutley Baptist Church, Plymouth, who first heard this material in sermon form and helped give it shape and colour.

To three colleagues whose administrative gifts are a great deal better than mine will ever be; Sonya Fisher, Helen Kinsman and Mary Tollins.

To my friend, Kim Bush, who has a keen eye and thoughtful heart.

To Mark Finnie at STL, and Steven May-Miller of Spring Harvest for working hard to allow this book see light of day. And to Alison Hull for her editorial skills.

To my friends, Brian and Eileen Phillips, for the loan of their haven in beautiful, rural France.

To Ruth – my life partner and most faithful critic. The shared journey gets better and better.

Finally, to King David – who continues to fascinate me by his hunger, holiness and humanity.

Introduction

It was a lovely summer's day, a date in the calendar that had long been eagerly anticipated. All the local schools had gathered for the district sports. I was thirteen years old and overjoyed to be running in the 100 yards race. Then a crisis occurred that would spoil my perfect day. One of our best runners, due to represent the school in the one mile event, called in sick. A replacement had to be found quickly – I don't know why they picked me. Without a word of coaching, I lined up at the start, surrounded by lads who were the finest in their school for this distance. I felt very inadequate – but did my best not to show it.

The starter's gun fired and we were off. I had no time to think. And that was where my problems began. I knew how to run – that was straightforward enough – but I had no real concept of how to run a mile in a competitive race.

I set off at a reasonable pace but noticed that no-one wanted to join me – by the end of the first lap I was a good 200 yards up on the rest. I felt good and the cheers of the crowd urged me forward. The second lap was not as easy as the first, and I could feel my legs getting heavier and my breathing more strained. But I held on and maintained a large lead.

By lap 3 my sports teacher ran alongside me for a short while, shouting his encouragement – he had a sort of wild-eyed look about him, almost as if he realised he might have

unwittingly found a future Olympic champion. Then everything began to seize up. That is the only way to describe it. My
brain knew what to do; it knew I was over half-way, in the
lead and just needed to keep going. But my brain and the rest
of my body were arguing. Various bits of me – quite simply –
refused to play any more. My brain kept barking out its orders
but the rest of me was not even listening.

If you have ever watched a battery toy slowly run down
and eventually stop, you have a good idea of what happened
next.

I stopped.

Suddenly.

The field had been gaining on me for some minutes and at
the exact moment the two lead runners caught up, I sank to
the ground in total collapse. To add injury to insult, the two
ran over me with their spiked shoes. There I lay, a punctured
and battered wreck.

Yes, the crowd was kind. My team mates were full of admiration, my sports teacher congratulated me for trying and I did
enjoy the celebrity status for the few days the news shot round
school. I was a loser but a bit of a hero for at least trying.

But nothing could take away that deep down sinking feeling that I had failed.

I learned a hard won lesson that day. It's one I have often
revisited over the intervening years.

If you want to run a long way you need a lot of puff.

My mistake was to treat a distance race as a sprint. It was a
big mistake to make and it ties in with Christian discipleship.
Following Jesus is about long distance running – but when we
treat it as a sprint, we hit problems.

Spirituality, in its many coloured forms is all the rage. But
what does it mean to be spiritual? What kind of spirituality is
attractive to the God who made us to know him?

There is a man who is described as being after God's own
heart.[1] In other words, his spirituality was something God
recognised, praised and held up as an example to follow. That
man was King David, and this book is a small attempt to
examine his story.

It might be helpful if a word of explanation is offered about how this book came to be written. As a leader in a local church, part of my responsibility is to teach the Bible in language that people can understand. I decided to teach through the life of David for a number of reasons:

- Apart from Jesus, no other character in the Bible occupies as much space as King David. The Bible treats him as important so his life must be worthy of serious study.
- King David's reign was seen as a high spot in the history of the nation of Israel. The importance of Jerusalem – the city of David – is just one example of his abiding influence in the modern state of Israel.
- David ranks among the great leaders of world history; as a military commander and politician he has been placed alongside Alexander the Great, Julius Caesar and Napoleon Bonaparte.[2]
- David plays an important role in the family line of Jesus – who was not ashamed to be known as 'the Son of David'. There are fifty-eight references in the New Testament to David, so the first followers of Jesus saw him as a significant figure in their story.
- The promise given to David that his line would not come to an end signals an important moment in biblical prophecy. Clearly David's line has ended, so how do we make sense of this statement?
- David is called the man after God's heart so his life must reveal something of the sort of spirituality that is attractive to the Lord.

These were a few of the important issues on my mind as I set out to preach a series of sermons on the life of David. It took me almost a whole year to complete and I became increasingly captivated by this fascinating man. I became so caught up in reading and reflecting, I didn't even care if no-one turned up to hear the sermon. Fortunately they did and – like me – many were captivated by David as well.

But this book is not a collection of sermons. It happened the other way round.

I decided to study David's life and write this book chapter by chapter. Then I preached to my congregation. Like many preachers, I have discovered that sermons have a life of their own. And so, based on watching and listening to how people responded, I went back to the chapters that had been written, tightening the text.

This book is not a scholarly treatment of the life of Israel's greatest king, but a straightforward attempt by a jobbing pastor to unpack David's fascinating story and help earth it in a twenty-first century world.

To that end each chapter has two main sections:

Listening to the story

This is a re-telling of the biblical narrative in a way that I hope will take the reader back to the text itself. The chapters are littered with footnotes for that very reason. The Bible is a powerful book that speaks better than any other. The David story is best read there.

Learning from the story

This deals with what I call the 'so what?' factor. David's story is more than a fascinating piece of historical biography. It explains how we can be people after God's heart. It is not a story of perfection – anything but. Part of David's magnetic pull is because of his flawed humanity. When we look at his life it is like looking in a mirror. We have much to learn from his triumphs and his failures.

In looking at David's life I have made a conscious effort to avoid airbrushing the picture painted by the Bible. As I have studied and preached through David's life, I have been reminded of the famous story about Oliver Cromwell. He sat for a portrait painted by Peter Lely, an artist with a formidable reputation. Most of his subjects had been the handsome courtiers of Charles I. Cromwell, by all accounts, was less attractive. He gave the artist a solemn charge,

> Mr Lely, I desire you would use all your skill to paint my picture truly like me, and not flatter me at all, but remark all these roughnesses, pimples, warts and everything as you see me, otherwise I will never pay a farthing for it.

And so, it is claimed, the phrase 'warts and all' became common currency for telling it like it is. That is what I have attempted to do with the Bible's portrait of David – to simply tell it like it is.

As a result there are parts of the story that still leave me puzzled. They may do the same for you.

But, overall, David's story has made me hungry for God.

May it do the same for you.

---

[1] 1 Samuel 13:14.

[2] This comparison has been made by Sir Fred Catherwood, former Vice-President of the European Parliament, in his study on the life of David. As a politician he offers the following comment. 'As one engaged in the great attempt to find ways of binding the twelve warring tribes of Western Europe into a peaceful confederation, I have found a study of David's success in binding – and keeping – the twelve tribes of Israel together very helpful. His patience, especially, is a lesson for us as he faced the instinctive separatism of "To your tents, O Israel!"; a call which has a very contemporary ring!' Sir Fred Catherwood, *David – Poet, Warrior, King* (Leicester: IVP, 1993), pp7, 15.

1

Called

Listening to the story – 1 Samuel 16:1-13

It is late afternoon and the sun is still burning in the sky. The old man makes his way slowly along the road that leads to the village – it is too hot to rush. Over his shoulder is slung a large bundle, held securely by his strong hand. His other hand grasps a rope, leading a young cow that follows meekly behind.

Some boys from the village are the first to spot the stranger. A couple of them run to greet him and prod with their curious questions. The man tells them to tell the elders his name and that he wants to see them. The boys speed away, leaving the man to continue at his measured pace.

The news spreads like wildfire. It is a small place and this is a big announcement. The village elders hurriedly gather, several having been called in from the fields. They begin to speculate, 'What's the problem?' 'What have we done?'

The nervous posse edge along the main path to the fringe of the village. The elders fall to their knees and pay their proper respects. Then the chairman clears his throat and asks the question everyone in Bethlehem is wondering about. 'Honoured Sir, why are you here?' Samuel smiles, 'I have come in peace – together we shall share in a celebration to the great Yahweh and you will be my honoured guests!'

Samuel has been so preoccupied as he walked, he has forgotten the impact that a surprise visit from the prophet of the Lord could cause in a small community. His arrival could herald a strong message of judgement or the exposure of some awful sin that blighted the smile of God on the nation.

As people scurry to prepare for the service and the feast that would follow, Samuel is led to the shade of the trees at the centre of Bethlehem. Hurrying hands bring water, wine and a chair as the elders gather to discover more about this mysterious visit. They remain suspicious. Why would the mighty Samuel, Yahweh's servant, spend time with them? Isn't Samuel the chief advisor to King Saul? Are there not great affairs of state screaming for his attention? Why visit Bethlehem? Why come today?

But Samuel has his own questions. How is their health and the state of the harvest? Then questions about the village and their loyalty to Yahweh. All the news is good. Then he asks a question that seems to have special importance, 'Is there a man called Jesse who lives among you?' They reply that his farm is a few miles away. He is an honourable man, respected by the whole community. Samuel seems pleased by this news, especially when they confirm that Jesse has several sons working with him. Samuel asks that a special invitation be sent to Jesse and his family to share in the celebrations. They are to be the prophet's honoured guests and the service will not begin until they have arrived. A messenger is immediately sent and within two hours Jesse and sons bow low to the ground before Samuel.

After the service and the offering of the sacrifice, the feasting and celebrations begin. There have been many village festivals but this is one to remember. The famous Samuel has chosen to visit them for this special feast – although the air of mystery lingers. Could there be something else behind his sudden arrival in Bethlehem?

Samuel asks if he can meet privately with Jesse and his sons. Eliab, the eldest, stands first before him. The prophet eyes him steadily, gazing deep into his eyes but saying nothing. There is an embarrassing silence and Samuel looks lost in his thoughts, still staring at the man before him. Eventually, with a look of puzzlement, he signals to Eliab to resume his place. Then the second son, Abinadab, stands forward and once more the prophet studies him without comment. It is as if he has something important to say but can't find the start of the sentence. Abinadab is told to stand back and his brother, Shammah, presents himself for this strange, silent ritual of examination. Then comes Nethanel, Raddai, Ozem and finally Elihu.[1] The introductions complete, Jesse stands respectfully, waiting to see what the man of God wants next.

'Are these your only sons?' Samuel asks, sounding agitated. 'Yes, I mean no, my Lord,' Jesse stumbles over his reply. 'There is one more but he is just a boy, the baby. We left him back at the farm to tend the sheep.[2] Your visit is a complete surprise, sir. We had to drop everything. So we left the youngster behind to sort out the sheep.' Samuel's face lightens as though a great weight has lifted from his shoulders. 'Fetch him quickly!' he says firmly. 'We won't start until he gets here.'

Two of the brothers leave at once and find their young brother out in the field watching the sheep. They tell him the news and urge him to change his clothes – he has been summoned to meet the legendary Samuel.

As his three sons enter, Jesse declares, 'Honoured sir, may I present the youngest in our family. His name is David.' Jesse pushes the boy forward and David bows low before the man of God. Samuel's eyes never leave the lad's face.

The boy stands in the centre of a room full of men. Awkward and embarrassed, he is not sure if he is meant to do or say anything. Samuel takes his jar of anointing oil and raises it high above his head. 'The Lord Yahweh sent me here today on a special mission. What I am about to do is to remain a closely guarded secret until the time that Yahweh decrees. He has chosen this lad, David, to be king over his holy people Israel. God has rejected Saul and has chosen David. This holy oil is the sign and symbol of Yahweh's favoured anointing.'

Samuel's voice trembles as he speaks the solemn words, 'David, my child, the Lord has chosen you to be the shepherd of his people.'

A stillness embraces them all as David kneels and Samuel slowly pours the anointing oil over his head. They watch in reverent silence as the oil covers him, running down the sides of his face, drenching his robe and splashing the floor.

Then Samuel prays. It is a prayer that none will ever forget – least of all David.

He knelt a boy and arose a man – God's man.

Learning from the story

The story of David's secret anointing has three key characters bound up with it – two men and a boy. The men were Saul the king and Samuel the prophet, and the boy was the star – David. We learn some important lessons from their stories.

Saul – who was rejected

Saul was chosen by God as Israel's first king. In one of the saddest biographies recorded in the Bible, he moves from a promising start to a tragic end. In twenty-three chapters his spiritual and mental condition rapidly deteriorate. Someone who began as an impressive character without equal among his fellows ends up committing suicide, with his body publicly desecrated by his enemies.[3] He ascended to the throne at the age of thirty and reigned for over forty years.[4] Although his reign began with great optimism, Saul lacked the strength needed to be a godly king. His disobedience revealed a deep character weakness.[5] He was not prepared to do things God's way. Power went to Saul's head and God decided to remove power from him. In a sad indictment we read, 'The Lord was grieved that he had made Saul king over Israel.'[6] As one writer expressed it, 'Israel's tallest king finished up its greatest fool.'[7] Saul started well and was a man of great humility[8] who knew a rich anointing from God on his life.[9]

The lesson that stands out from Saul's sad story is that our actions have consequences. 'You reap what you sow' is a basic principle of life and it is a view endorsed by the Bible.[10] Some of us may presume that what the Bible says about God's forgiveness offers a licence to do what we like. But such a view fails to understand that we never walk away from sin unaffected. We may find forgiveness but we live with the consequences.

Samuel – who was dejected

In the story of Samuel anointing David as Saul's replacement, God asks Samuel a direct question, 'How long will you mourn for Saul, since I have rejected him as king over Israel?'[11] Samuel was deeply affected by Saul's failure.[12] The Lord's command to Samuel reveals something of the inner conflict the prophet suffered. Perhaps he felt some sense of personal failure because of Saul's disobedience. God was able to move on before Samuel did.

We can have unresolved issues and find ourselves frozen with grief. At such times we need to recall God's ability to move us forward and offer us hope. We can never move forward unless we are willing for God to bring closure to things that affect us.

David – who was selected

Samuel was an old man at the time David was anointed[13] and had lived through much as the Lord's servant – but there were still lessons to be learned. God sent him to Jesse's home because one of his sons would replace Saul as king. Following the culture and custom of his day, Samuel assumed that the eldest, Eliab, was the one the Lord had chosen. Then God made Samuel relearn a fundamental lesson: God looks at things differently from us. We are obsessed with the outer appearance, but God looks on the heart.[14]

What did God see in David that made him stand out from the crowd? Some point to the Psalms – his prayer songs – that reveal a hungry passion for God and a restless desire that all of David's life might be lived well under divine influence. God chose David and in so doing went against the accepted norms. Samuel had to learn (again) that God's ways are not our ways.

From this opening story in David's life we can discover four important lessons for life:

1. Don't leave God's pathway

Saul lost God's calling on his life. Disobedience has a price tag attached: we must read it carefully. The challenge to obey and follow Christ is a daily one. That is why the New Testament is filled with exhortations to make right choices. We are urged to 'put to death, therefore, whatever belongs to your earthly nature' and instead to 'clothe yourselves with compassion, kindness, humility, gentleness and patience'.[15]

It is hard to be holy and when we are tempted to quit the struggle, Saul's story reminds us of the consequences. God has not left us alone – a holy life is made possible only through the influence of the Holy Spirit. As we give ourselves over to his leading and control, we find a power to change that comes from outside ourselves.

2. Don't get trapped in the past

Samuel needed to hear God's invitation to move on. Past disappointments can stunt our growth. We can be trapped by resentment or an unforgiving spirit. Samuel's story reminds us that there are times when we simply need to move on. This is brought home by a powerful story told by Tony Campolo, detailing the first meeting between President Bill Clinton and Nelson Mandela. Clinton began by asking a searching question:

> 'When you were released from prison, Mr Mandela, I woke my daughter at three o'clock in the morning. I wanted her to see this historic event. As you marched from the cellblock across the yard to the gate of the prison, the camera focussed in on your face. I have never seen such anger, and even hatred, in any man as was

expressed on your face at that time. That's not the Nelson Mandela I know today. What was that all about?'

Mandela answered, 'I'm surprised that you saw that, and I regret that the cameras caught my anger. As I walked across the courtyard that day I thought to myself, "They've taken everything from you that matters. Your cause is dead. Your family is gone. Your friends have been killed. Now they're releasing you, but there is nothing left for you out there." And I hated them for what they had taken from me. Then I sensed an inner voice saying to me "Nelson! For twenty-seven years you were their prisoner, but you were always a free man! Don't allow them to make you into a free man, only to turn you into their prisoner!" [16]

Campolo concludes: 'An unforgiving spirit creates bitterness in our souls and imprisons our spirits. A failure to forgive imprisons us.'

The issue for Samuel was probably more to do with disappointment than unforgiveness. But he was still a prisoner. But as he obeyed God, he stopped living in the past and began living for the future.

3. Don't make superficial judgements

Samuel, as an old man, needed to relearn a lesson about how God works. He had to abandon superficial judgements – even socially acceptable ones – and see things as God does. We need that gift of discernment too. We can easily believe what we need to do is obvious, particularly if we have been Christians for some years. Because we have faced situations before, we can wrongly assume that our path will follow in the same direction. But Samuel's experience at Bethlehem reminds us that presumption is a dangerous thing.

Paul, the Christian leader, offered this prayer for a local church he had planted, 'that your love may abound more and more in knowledge and depth of insight, so that you may be able to discern what is best'.[17] Discerning what is best means taking time to seek God's will and avoiding the temptation of leaping to hasty conclusions.

4. Don't neglect the anointing

God chose David and anointed him with the Spirit. He gave him a job to do and the tools he needed. When Samuel anointed David's head and offered his prayer of dedication, he was confirming God's choice. This anointing was foundational in David's life. There was a long wait until he took the throne in place of Saul and those waiting years were part of God's preparation. But the anointing of God's Spirit never left him and the formation of character and development of gifts can be directly traced to this.

God gives his Holy Spirit to all who trust and follow Christ.[18] The Holy Spirit is the one who reveals that we belong in the family of God,[19] who helps us in our praying,[20] who produces godly character,[21] equips us with gifts[22] and leads us into truth.[23] We are exhorted to be filled continually with the Holy Spirit and never to tire of seeking God for more.[24] When asked why he needed to keep praying to be filled with the Holy Spirit, a seasoned Christian leader replied, 'Because I leak a lot!'

David's story reminds us of the constant need to be saturated with the Holy Spirit. God gives us his Spirit freely. Let us resist the temptation to live in our own strength. Live with the anointing.[25]

---

[1] 1 Chronicles 2:13-15 and 1 Chronicles 27:18 name these four sons.

[2] Eugene Petersen, *Leap Over A Wall* (San Francisco; Harper, 1997), p16. '(David) enters the story unnamed, dismissively referred to as "the baby brother" – in Hebrew, *haqqaton*, the youngest, in effect saying: "Well there's the baby brother, but he's out tending the sheep" (1 Sam. 16:11). If you're the youngest of seven brothers, you're probably never going to be thought of as other than the kid brother. *Haqqaton* carries undertones of insignificance, of not counting for very much – certainly not the prime candidate for prestigious work. The family runt.'

[3] The chapters detailing Saul's reign run from 1 Samuel 9 – 31. His physical appearance is described in 1 Samuel 9:2 in these words, 'an impressive young man without equal among the Israelites – a head taller than any of the others.'

4 1 Samuel 13:1 – although there is discussion over the accuracy of these dates, both Acts 13:21 and the Jewish historian, Josephus, suggest Saul reigned for forty years.

5 The details are recorded in 1 Samuel 13 – 15.

6 1 Samuel 15:35.

7 Raymond Brown, *Skilful Hands – Studies in the Life of David* (London: Lakeland, 1972), p16.

8 1 Samuel 9:21.

9 1 Samuel 10:10.

10 Galatians 6:7.

11 1 Samuel 16:1.

12 1 Samuel 15:24-35.

13 1 Samuel 12:2.

14 1 Samuel 16:7.

15 Colossians 3:5, 12.

16 Tony Campolo, *Let me Tell You A Story* (W. Publishing Group, 2000), p66-7.

17 Philippians 1:9-10.

18 Romans 5:1-5.

19 Galatians 4:6-7.

20 Romans 8:26-27.

21 Galatians 5:16-26.

22 1 Corinthians 12:1-11.

23 John 14:25-26.

24 Ephesians 5:18.

25 1 John 2:20, 27.

2

Fighter

Listening to the story – 1 Samuel 17:28-58

The man is big – around three metres tall. He is strong – his body armour alone weighs almost sixty kilos. He carries the biggest spear anyone has seen. He is a one-man army, a walking, talking, mountain of terror.[1]

His name is Goliath from Gath, the land of the Philistine people. He is their hero, a champion fighter who has never been beaten. You only have to see him to understand why.

It is the same this particular morning as it has been every day for the past six weeks. An army made up of Israel's finest fighting men, under the command of King Saul, is locked in a stalemate with the Philistine army ranged against them on the other side of the Elah Valley.

It is a stand-off, in military terms – the army of Israel on a hill to the north, the Philistines on the southern slopes opposite and a great valley between.[2] Neither want to attack. Every day both armies muster on their hillsides. The men line up and begin shouting and banging shields, but neither side makes a move. After some time, the shouting dies down, both sides post guards, and the bulk of the fighting soldiers slip away out of the heat of the sun, until it begins to sink in the sky. As the evening shadows begin to fall, the armies reassemble and the whole performance starts again until everyone decides enough is enough. Morning and evening, the fearsome Goliath makes an appearance and throws out a challenge for the army of Israel to choose a champion to fight him.

Rumours are rife. The story in the Israeli camp is that the opposition is waiting for more forces to arrive. The Philistines are surprised that King Saul has raised such a large force to repel their invasion and they need some back-up – so the daily Goliath performance is a massive propaganda coup. The longer it runs, the more chance they have of reinforcements arriving.

Goliath's intimidation routine has been effective in demoralising Israel's troops. It is the same morning and evening, Goliath steps forward and shouts his challenge across the valley: 'Men of Israel, choose a champion! Let him fight me and whoever wins decides this matter between us. If he kills me, then we Philistines will serve you. But if I kill him, then you must accept defeat and become our slaves. Come on, choose your best man and let him fight me now!'[3]

Day after day it goes on, the same speech – and the same result. No-one wants to fight him. The rumours say no-one could fight him and live. The taunting gets louder. The tactics seem to be working – the whole army of Israel, from the commander to the lowliest soldier, is terrified.[4]

Then something happens that changes everything.

One day a young Israeli boy comes into the camp. His family run a farm near Bethlehem, about fifteen miles away. He has visited his three brothers in the Israeli army several times. His father sends them food. On this particular day, he arrives in the camp while both armies are assembling for the morning shouting match. Leaving the food with the quartermaster, the lad goes to the front line to find his brothers. No sooner has he found them than Goliath starts his daily defiant ritual: 'Send out a champion to fight me. What's the matter? Haven't you got anyone? Aren't any of you man enough?'

The jeering from the Philistines becomes louder as they curse their opponents. Fear runs through the Israeli lines: will the waiting game soon end? When the extra Philistine troops arrive, there will be no hope of holding them – it will be a bloodbath. Many men are scared for their families, knowing exactly what the Philistines can do.

Part of their insecurity is because they lack a proper leader. Saul may be king, but he has lost his way. He had enjoyed popular public support. Israel had become like the other nations with a proper king. But Saul has lost ground and the nation desperately needs leadership.

The army of Israel faces an imminent massacre, when the word goes round that someone has volunteered to take up Goliath's challenge. Speculation spreads rapidly: who is foolhardy enough to face such a powerful fighter? What is his name? Where does he come from? There is a buzz of excitement when word goes out that the volunteer hero has gone to King Saul's tent.

Whoever has come forward, they are inside the tent for ages – some high-level discussions are taking place. The men draw closer to see who will emerge. Who should step out of the king's tent but the young lad who has come to the camp on a family errand – he isn't even an enlisted soldier! Then someone shouts, 'Where are your weapons? You can't fight Goliath like that!' The lad points to the sling in his belt. 'This is Yahweh's war,' he says. 'He will bring victory that is not to do with weapons. The Lord will give us victory today!'

There is something about his voice, the way he looks, that make it all sound possible. The silent army watch its surprising hero as he clambers down the slope to the valley floor. He looks like a lamb heading for slaughter.

It is later that the full story emerges. The lad's offer is accepted by Saul, and his advisers insist that he is properly equipped. The royal armour is brought – after all, the king's champion should at least dress the part. But the armour is clumsy – the boy is a shepherd, not a soldier. He asks to face Goliath in his own way and puts up a persuasive case. His shepherding work with the family's flocks has taught him some skills, especially with the sling. He has killed lions and bears, the speed of his feet and the sharpness of his shot protecting him. Winning the argument, he faces Goliath with nothing more than a staff, a sling and the clothes he stands up in. Down in the valley, he picks up a handful of stones.

Goliath is *not* impressed. He comes down from the Philistine camp shouting at the top of his voice. He is angry. Who do they think he is – some mad dog that can be chased off with a stick? Is this some kind of joke that the Israelis are having at his expense? He tells the lad he is going to tear him apart limb from limb and leave his carcass for the birds to feed on.

The lad doesn't seem worried but he does look small. He shouts back at Goliath 'You have come against me with weapons but I come in the name of Yahweh the God of Israel. He is the one you have defied and laughed at. Today you will die because Yahweh has given you into my hands. You and your army will perish. This battle belongs to God!'[5]

What happens next has gone down in history as one of the most remarkable, unpredictable occurrences in warfare. The lad has taken one of the stones from his pocket and loaded his catapult. As Goliath moves down the track towards him, he takes aim. Letting the sling fly round his head, he lets go. This stone flies through the air and hits Goliath in the middle of his forehead. It is a perfect shot! There is a loud crack and Goliath stands still, sways for a moment and then falls flat on his face, knocked out cold. Quick as a flash, the lad rushes over to the man and draws his massive sword, plunging it into him one, two, three times. A deafening roar rises from the ranks of Israel as they watch Goliath die before their eyes.

The Philistines are thrown into confusion. With their champion dead and reinforcements a long way off, they run for their lives. The Israeli army chases the fleeing Philistines all the way back to the cities of Gath and Ekron. The Philistine army is routed and their camp plundered.

This is a day when history has been written. A teenage shepherd boy has defeated a giant of a man, a professional soldier. Israel has seen certain massacre turn into remarkable victory in the space of a few hours. No-one would have predicted the outcome – except possibly the young lad. People recall the look in his eyes as he made his way to meet Goliath.

The lad becomes a hero. David is his name. David, the youngest son of Jesse from Bethlehem. A name to remember – and a man to watch.

Learning from the story

The story of David and Goliath speaks directly into our lives today. It is more than a story to occupy children in a Sunday school class. It holds vital principles about the life of faith. We face giants just as terrifying as Goliath. They may not wear armour and shout but they disturb our peace and challenge our progress as disciples of Christ.

Giants come in various shapes and sizes. Fear, unbelief, temptation, a lack of self-worth or a particular challenge that we face can all take on enormous proportions.

David's response to the defiant challenge of Goliath teaches some important truths about fighting giants – and winning.

David was willing to fight

Everyone else backed away but David is prepared to fight. Several times over in the story, David makes it clear that this Philistine is defying Yahweh.[6] This is no mere teenager whose mouth is bigger than his brain. This is a response born of spiritual maturity and courage. David has been anointed to lead so it is hardly surprising that, faced with adversity, he begins to live out his calling.

When we face 'giants' we need to resist the longing to run away. The determination to face an issue is step one on the road to winning. Many of us make the mistake of thinking that courage means the absence of fear. Far from it, courage is about facing fear and bringing it under control. The most frequent command in the Bible is not (as some might imagine) 'Don't sin' or even 'Be good'. The command that is repeated most is 'Fear not!' When we face our fears with faith, we are simply doing as we are told. We need to have the desire to fight and win. As Jesus challenged the man who was paralysed, he challenges us to move beyond living in a permanent state of defeat.[7]

David faced this battle on the basis of past experience

God wastes none of his children's experience, including their pain and tears. When Saul told David that his desire to fight Goliath was not founded in reality, he was countered by the voice of experience. David was young (probably a teenager) but he had faced a few experiences in life. He had faced both a lion and a bear when tending his family's herd.[8] Out of these potentially traumatic experiences had come a refined courage. The Lord had helped him in the past and his grace was exactly the same for this current crisis. The face of the enemy might have changed – but the principle remained the same. The Lord stands ready to help all those who cast themselves on him.

We are also reminded of the importance of memory. When we are attacked, the memory is often the enemy's first target. We forget that we have been this way before and seen the deliverance of God. It was David who expressed this in one of his own songs of worship to Yahweh:

> Praise the Lord, O my soul
> and forget not all his benefits –
> who forgives all your sins
> and heals all your diseases,
> who redeems your life from the pit
> and crowns you with love and compassion,
> who satisfies your desires with good things
> so that your youth is renewed like the eagle's.[9]

We do well to 'forget not all his benefits' because prayers answered yesterday fuel faith for those offered today.

David refused to rely on the best human weapons

David rejected Saul's armour because it didn't fit him. It failed to meet the need David had as he fought Goliath. Hand-to-hand combat requires as much protection as possible. But this was not the method by which the Lord would defeat Goliath. The sling and handful of stones were God's tactics for this giant. This underlines the need for us to look to God alone for wisdom and for weapons.

Paul knew this when he wrote these words, 'The weapons we fight with are not the weapons of the world. On the contrary, they have divine power to demolish strongholds.'[10] There are occasions when we make the mistake of relying on our own resources. Letting God choose the weapons is always the wisest solution.

David faced Goliath with absolute faith in God

There is something powerful and prophetic in David's challenge to Goliath. This man had taunted the army of Israel for six long weeks. Behind his taunting was a mocking spirit that stood opposed to Yahweh. David spotted the issue for what it was; 'Who is this uncircumcised Philistine that he should defy the armies of the living God?'[11] David saw the disgrace this defiance brought to the name of the Lord. When he eventually confronted Goliath face to face, it is instructive to note how David challenged him,

'You come against me with sword and spear and javelin, but I come against you in the name of the Lord Almighty, the God of the armies of Israel, whom you have defied.

This day the Lord will hand you over to me, and I'll strike you down and cut off your head. Today I will give the carcasses of the Philistine army to the birds of the air and the beasts of the earth, and the whole world will know that there is a God in Israel.

All those gathered here will know that it is not by sword or spear that the Lord saves; for the battle is the Lord's, and he will give all of you into our hands.'[12]

David's words are not full of himself – rather they are full of the Lord. It is in his name and in his power that the victory will come.

David gave glory to God for his victory

One of the things that marks David as a man after God's heart[13] is his great love for God and his capacity for worship. Supremely, this is reflected in the many psalms he wrote, preserved for us in the Old Testament. There is a psalm-like quality about his challenge to Goliath, '…it is not by sword or spear that the Lord saves; for the battle is the Lord's, and he will give all of you into our hands'.[14]

David is giving glory to God before his battle with Goliath has started! When we read the psalms of David, we gain insight into the inner workings of his heart. Many of them were written at times of personal need – sometimes in the midst of great crisis. They reflect the mind of a man of faith and shine a light on our own pathway in all the seasons of the soul.[15]

Eugene Petersen sums up David's insatiable appetite for God in these words:

> In the Bethlehem hills and meadows, tending his father's sheep, David was immersed in the largeness and immediacy of God. He had experienced God's strength in protecting the sheep in his fights with lions and bears. He had practised the presence of God so thoroughly that God's word, which he couldn't literally hear, was far more real to him than the lion's roar, which he could hear. He had worshipped the majesty of God so continuously that God's love, which he couldn't see, was far more real to him than the bear's ferocity, which he could see. His praying and singing, his meditation and adoration had shaped an imagination in him that set each sheep and lamb, bear and lion into something large and vast and robust: God.[16]

In the spiritual life, worshippers always make the best warriors.

---

[1] 1 Samuel 17:4-7.

[2] 1 Samuel 17:1-3.

[3] 1 Samuel 17:8-10.

4   1 Samuel 17:11.

5   1 Samuel 17:45-47.

6   1 Samuel 17:26, 36, 45.

7   John 5:1ff.

8   1 Samuel 17:34-36.

9   Psalm 103:1-5.

10   2 Corinthians 10:4.

11   1 Samuel 17:26.

12   1 Samuel 17:45-47.

13   David is often called 'the man after God's heart' and this is based on a phrase used by the prophet Samuel when he confronted Saul over his disobedience and tells him God had chosen another to be king over Israel. See 1 Samuel 13:14.

14   1 Samuel 17:47.

15   See, for example, the words of Psalm 25 in which David seeks God's protection, guidance and forgiveness. Each verse begins with successive letters of the Hebrew alphabet, indicating that it was composed with thought and skill. David's faith was neither mindless, careless nor sentimental. These rivers ran deep.

16   Petersen, *Leap Over A Wall*, p40.

3

Enemy

Listening to the story – 1 Samuel 16:14-23, 18:5-16

Saul's sad life can be summed up in one phrase: 'How the mighty have fallen!'[1] He starts his reign full of promise. Samuel brings him before the people and announces him as Yahweh's chosen one. But his early promise turns to deep disappointment. He misses God's best through wilful and persistent disobedience.

There have been no obvious signs that his surprise elevation to the throne has gone to his head. He leads the people in some successful military campaigns against Israel's enemies – first the Ammonites[2] and then the Philistines.[3] Other military victories follow and Saul establishes himself as a strong and capable king.[4] Alongside his undoubted military strength, he displays shrewdness in his political judgements. When a group among the Israelites refuse to accept 'this Benjaminite' and insult him by withholding a coronation gift, Saul shows remarkable restraint in not giving his opponents a greater platform than their cause deserves.[5]

But soon the cracks begin to show. Saul demonstrates on two separate occasions that he sees Yahweh as more of a commodity to be used than a Sovereign to be served. Saul's belief in God is superficial and immature. God doesn't figure highly in Saul's affections or plans – and it shows.

The first incident occurs during a military campaign against the Philistines. Samuel has ordered Saul not to fight until he arrives to make offerings and prayers. When Samuel doesn't appear on time, Saul makes the act of dedication himself, moving beyond his calling, anointing and authority.[6] Samuel then announces that God will replace Saul as king by 'a man after his own heart'.[7]

The second incident again revolves around Saul's disobedience to a direct instruction from God. The Amalekites are to be totally destroyed but Saul, for political rather than humanitarian reasons, decides to amend the order. When confronted by Samuel he lies, before (reluctantly) acknowledging his sin.[8] This shows Saul's pragmatism could prove fatal to the nation. Samuel issues Yahweh's stark decision. Saul has rejected the word of the Lord – so Yahweh has rejected him as king.[9]

Saul's life now takes a steep downward turn and he is often deeply depressed. Wracked by guilt and failure, he becomes introvert and dangerously moody. He has lost God's anointing and, in the vacuum, many dark and damaging thoughts make their nest.

Those closest to him, alarmed by the mood swings and violent outbursts, decide on some music therapy. A musician who can play the harp and bring some relief to Saul's savage moods is found. David is appointed to the court of King Saul as musician in residence. His playing is skilful enough to bring a sense of peace to Saul, who promotes him within the palace staff.[10]

It is around this time that David (probably before his full-time appointment in the palace) challenges the Philistine Goliath and opens the way for Israel to defeat his army. This secures David a promotion into the army of Israel as a commander. His popularity increases and he becomes a national hero, even featuring in a folk song that makes up part of the massive celebrations for the defeat of the Philistines. The women sing, 'Saul has slain his thousands and David his tens of thousands.'[11]

At one level this joy is a good thing. The mood in Israel has been sombre. They know what a successful Philistine invasion would mean – rape, torture, enslavement and death. There are deep insecurities about King Saul. The confident military com-mander who has led them to some great victories seems hesitant and confused. When the Philistine champion Goliath challenged the Israeli army every day for six weeks, Saul sat in his tent, doing nothing. Rumours abound about Samuel. Once Saul's mentor, now he never comes near the king. There is even public talk about Saul's dark depressions.

These have been uncertain times in Israel but now, at last, some good news. Victory has come. A new young hero, David from Bethlehem, brings hope. But this national mood of joy is not shared by all. Saul is furious when he hears the words of the song. Does it not claim that David is ten times the man he is? Into an already troubled mind, some jealous seeds are sown. No doubt Saul has mentally revisited his final meeting with Samuel, replaying the fateful words, 'The Lord has rejec-ted you as king over Israel.'[12] Saul knows that he is not merely rejected – but will be replaced.[13]

In his jealous paranoia, Saul looks at David and sees a rival who surely must be eyeing the throne. He is now the enemy.[14] It is against this background that a disturbing incident occurs.

Saul is in his palace, engaged in some spiritual exercise, possibly trying to rebuild his relationship with Yahweh. But it isn't helping his mood. He is deeply depressed and angry. His attendants call for David to play some music, without realis-ing that his very presence will only inflame Saul further.

Saul hears the music from his inner chamber and knows at once it is David – the one who will snatch his throne. The fury that has smouldered for days suddenly erupts and Saul, with shouts and curses, rushes from his bedroom, grabbing a spear as he runs. David stops playing and looks up in time to see Saul, incandescent with rage, hurl the spear across the room. David runs. The spear crashes against the wall where he has been sitting, embedding itself deeply. Running across the room, David can hear Saul shouting louder. As he reaches the main doorway, David is confronted by the king, another spear in his hand. Saul unleashes the weapon with a cry of fury. The missile whistles through the air and David manages to make it through the door as the second spear sticks into the wall.[15]

The palace officials try to hush things up, of course. It is made clear that incidents of this nature are not to become common knowledge. But people talk and draw their own conclusions. An apology is offered to David and accepted, some smoothing of the way takes place by those skilled in such matters of fine politics. But no explanation is given as to why the king's dark moods are now turning to outbreaks of violence and why one of the brightest and most popular young men in the nation should almost have been murdered.

In an attempt to keep David sweet, a hasty promotion is arranged. David will take charge of a regiment of a thousand men, engaging in military duties well away from the palace, minimising the chances of another unfortunate incident. David's career takes off. He is popular with his officers and men and whatever he tackles goes well. The Lord's hand is on David – and it shows. Meanwhile, back at the palace, Saul is deeply afraid of David. Something burns deep inside – an insane jealousy that dominates his waking hours and torments him at night. It is a thought that continually nags at the edges of his mind. David will be king one day.

Learning from the story

Others have drawn attention to the fact that the Bible paints portraits of Saul and David that provide stark contrasts. Alan Redpath puts it well:

> Quite clearly, at this point of the story, the Holy Spirit brings to our attention David and Saul, setting them side by side for our careful, thoughtful meditation. Both of them were chosen for leadership and both of them were anointed by the Spirit. But with those two statements comparison ceases and contrast begins, for everything else in the life of Saul and David is in striking opposition. We see the sun begin to rise upon one life and to set upon the other. For one, there is steady growth in grace and in the knowledge of God;

for the other there is tragic decline and disobedience to God: darkness, frustration, sin.[16]

This contrast can be expressed in two phrases,

- Saul and missing God's best
- David and pursuing God's best

Saul and missing God's best

Three lessons stand out from this sad episode in Saul's
decline. He had failed to live up to his early promise. Saul is
not alone in this, as Jesus showed in the Parable of the
Sower.[17] It is possible to begin to follow Christ and then get
distracted, discouraged or completely diverted. Paul, the
Christian leader, threw out a challenge to a first-century
group of believers along similar lines: 'You were running a
good race. Who cut in on you and kept you from obeying the
truth?'[18]

How had Saul gone off course? His life illustrates three
principles taught in Scripture:

• *Obedience is better than sacrifice*

This statement is a direct quotation from Samuel when he
denounced Saul's disobedience and informed him he would
be replaced as king over Israel. In fact the whole of Samuel's
prophetic declaration is worthy of study.[19] Saul was religious
in that he would offer his sacrifices to God but in his immatu-
rity of faith, he failed to understand that the greatest gift we
bring to God is our obedience. He was willing to go along with
the externals of religion but not to get personally involved.
The gifts and sacrificial offerings that Saul brought were a
smokescreen for an unsurrendered heart. Such rebellion in
God's eyes is as bad as engaging in occult practice. Saul's
example serves as a warning against superficiality when it
comes to matters of faith. God seeks obedience – nothing more
nor less.

● *The wages of sin is death*

This well-known New Testament statement[20] is often taken to refer to the consequences of sin, resulting in eternal separation from God's holy presence. That solemn truth must be an essential part of any teaching of the gospel that accords with orthodox understanding of the Christian faith. But sin's wages do not wait for us only beyond death. It makes some substantial advance payments this side of eternity.

The writer of 1 Samuel talks about an evil spirit from God tormenting Saul.[21] That does not mean that God sent a demonic spirit into Saul's life. God is not the author of evil nor does he support its cause. But the writer is trying hard to express in words and thoughts this enormous change that took place in Saul's life when he moved away from God's will. He lost the anointing of the Spirit of God and into that vacuum another spirit came. It was dark and destructive – 'evil' in every way. The writer could not comprehend anything like this happening without God's express permission, so in this sense it was 'sent' by the Lord. Saul's disobedience paid a dividend. So does ours.

● *Beware the root of bitterness*

Saul's sad life illustrates the importance of dealing with basic things such as bitterness, jealousy and the desire for revenge. By neglecting to deal with them, they get worse. Nowhere does the Scripture speak of Saul repenting, praying or seeking help. He ended up where he did by doing nothing. The answer to our need so often begins with our willingness to own up to our need.

What starts as a small issue in a person's life can, if left untended, grow larger. Saul's resentment about David's popularity continued unchecked until, in a jealous fit of rage, he tried to kill him. The angry outburst could have been stopped at its source but Saul chose to ignore the wrong feelings.

The lesson is plain – deal with wrong feelings swiftly and tackle breaches in relationships without delay. Otherwise wounds can become infected with poison.

David and pursuing God's best

What a contrast in David's young life. He had been secretly anointed by Samuel as the replacement to Saul and found himself serving at the royal palace and doing an apprenticeship he could not have organised better for himself. David reveals three principles for those who want God's best and are committed to seeking first the Kingdom in all their dealings.[22]

● *The best leaders are servants*

David could have been consumed with a lust for power – after all, he had been chosen by God to rule on Saul's throne. But instead he took the place of a servant in the royal palace – and his job was not the most glamorous or secure! A willingness to serve – and do whatever you are asked to do – are key indicators of how well someone will lead.

As a leader in a local church, I am often approached to supply a reference for one of our members applying to enrol at theological college or to work with a mission agency. The questions on the form are so similar I know what I will be asked – one will be: 'please give details about how the candidate has been serving in your church'. What evidence is there that this person has understood what service and servanthood are about? Faithfulness in small things is the prerequisite for being entrusted with greater responsibilities.[23]

● *The importance of waiting for God's timing*

An underlying theme of David's story was his willingness to wait for God's timing. He approached life with an overarching sense of the plan of God. David turned down every opportunity to engineer and fix things for himself. Instead he was content to rest in God and, as many of his psalms point out, he was confident that the Lord's plans for his life would come to pass. David knew God's timing was perfect and that he would lead him in the right pastures at the right time.[24]

What a contrast this poses in our do-it-yourself, quick-fix
culture! David's trust in God went beyond catchy lyrics – it
was expressed by the way he lived.

● *With the anointing comes opposition*

David reveals an important truth of the life of faith. Paul tells
Timothy, a young church leader: 'Everyone who wants to live
a godly life in Christ Jesus will be persecuted.'[25]

This does not mean that we should go looking for it – but it
does mean we should not be surprised when opposition rears
its ugly head. David experienced enormous opposition before
he reached the throne. Even then the opposition didn't
completely vanish, it simply changed clothes. Paul's wise
words bear thoughtful reflection. Anyone who seeks to live a
counter-culture life will experience opposition. The scale may
vary from sarcastic humour to imprisonment and death. But
opposition is par for the course.

I recently watched a film detailing the training of troops
chosen to serve in the SAS. They were subject to the most
rigorous tests, including having to withstand capture and
interrogation. When questioned about the validity of what
appeared to be licensed brutality, the officer in charge replied,
'This is what they are going to face and we need to know if
they can stand it.'

David's anointing attracted opposition. We need to understand that the more we give ourselves to God and seek to live
by his standards, the more we too will face challenges. Then
we need to recall that the Spirit of God living within us means
that opposition should be expected.

If you are living under God's anointing and pursuing his
best – it goes with the territory.

---

[1] Taken from David's song of lament, written to commemorate the
death of Saul and his son, Jonathan. 2 Samuel 1:19.

[2] 1 Samuel 11:1ff.

[3] 1 Samuel 13:1ff.

[4] 1 Samuel 14:47-48.

5   1 Samuel 10:26-27.

6   1 Samuel 13:1ff and Saul's pathetic and pragmatic defence in vv11-12.

7   1 Samuel 13:14.

8   1 Samuel 15:1ff.

9   Samuel's uncompromising verdict in 1 Samuel 15:17-35.

10 1 Samuel 16:14-23.

11 1 Samuel 18:7.

12 1 Samuel 15:26.

13 1 Samuel 13:13-14.

14 1 Samuel 18:8-9.

15 1 Samuel 18:10-11.

16 Alan Redpath, *The Making of A Man of God* (Michigan: Fleming H. Revell, 2000), p31.

17 Matthew 13:1-23.

18 Galatians 5:7.

19 1 Samuel 15:22-23.

20 Romans 6:23.

21 1 Samuel 16:14.

22 Matthew 6:33.

23 Matthew 25:21.

24 Psalm 23.

25 2 Timothy 3:12.

4

Friend

Listening to the story –
1 Samuel 18:1-4, 2 Samuel 1:17-27

You can tell much about a person by their friends. We know from experience that good friends can enrich us as much as bad friends can hinder us. The David story is not just about the jealous, insane anger of Saul. There are some bright spots in the tale. One of the brightest is the unique friendship shared between David and Saul's son, Jonathan. Their friendship begins when David rises to public prominence, following the Goliath episode. As his fame and popularity begin to spread, David moves into the palace permanently and, under Saul's express orders, becomes a military commander.[1]

The friendship – at least on Jonathan's part – is marked by four features:

1. Admiration

Jonathan respects David as a warrior. Not short on courage himself, his own exploits against the Philistines (long before David arrived on the scene) have not gone unnoticed.[2] How easy it would have been for Jonathan to be filled with jealousy at David's exploits. Instead there is intense admiration from one warrior towards another.

2. Humility

Jonathan is heir to his father's throne. He could easily have seen David as a potential threat to his accession but seems oblivious of this. When his father Saul points out to Jonathan that David will prevent him rising to power,[3] he is more concerned about Saul's appalling behaviour towards David. For Jonathan, relationships appear to be of higher value than personal success or power. These are the actions of a humble man.

3. Generosity

Jonathan gives David his own robe, tunic, sword, bow and belt.[4] These are symbolic and precious gifts, for Jonathan is a royal prince and these things mark out his status. By giving them to David, he is making a statement about his depth of commitment. Some would go further and see in this gift a prophetic act in which Jonathan 'hands over' the throne to David in recognition that he will follow Saul as the next king over Israel.

4. Commitment

Jonathan makes a covenant with David although we are not told its exact terms.[5] Later in the story this contract is re-affirmed when the situation worsens, from David's point of view, as Saul's hatred against him intensifies.[6] This agreement is based on Jonathan's deep desire to affirm his loyalty to David, perhaps anticipating the battle for the throne that lies ahead.

The quality of the friendship between David and Jonathan is illustrated in two episodes, one from each side of the relationship.

● *Episode 1 – True friendship has strong shoulders*

Saul's insane rage against David has reached boiling point. The king conspires to murder David but Jonathan talks his father round. After a temporary lull, in another moment of madness, Saul tries to kill David. So great is the risk that David flees from the palace at night and goes into hiding. [7]

David sends a message to his friend Jonathan and they meet together secretly and review the deterioration in Saul's attitude.[8] David is convinced Saul is out to kill him – but Jonathan takes a different tack. Believing he can talk his father round again, he assures David that the king would do nothing without including Jonathan in his plans. David is less convinced – having become adept at dodging Saul's spears. He comes up with a plan to test the situation, which Jonathan readily agrees to adopt.

A New Moon festival is due, running for several days. It is customary for the entire royal household to attend the various evening banquets. Usually, David would be present at the king's table as an army commander. Reluctant to attend – for obvious reasons – David agrees with Jonathan that Saul's reaction to his absence would provide the indicator the two of them sought. They agree a code to convey the test results. It is too risky for them to meet openly until they know the king has changed his attitude towards David.

They agree to meet at a certain location in a few days' time, surrounded with the utmost secrecy, as both will be vulnerable to arrest for what could appear to be a 'treasonable act'. Jonathan will pretend to do some archery practice, with a young servant lad assisting. As he shoots the arrows, the lad will collect them. If Jonathan shoots short, that will be the signal that all is well with Saul and David can return safely to the palace. If, however, he shoots his arrows beyond the boy, that will be the sign that David is still at risk.

As they agree to this plan of action, they pledge themselves again to each other's welfare. This is no token gesture of friendship. In the normal course of events, another family, when taking over the throne, would eliminate all remnants of the old dynasty. The pledge of love and loyalty is of groundbreaking proportions.

The plan swings into action. The first evening of the festival arrives and David does not appear. Saul holds his counsel, believing he may have been legitimately detained. But on the second evening when David fails to appear, the king demands to know where he is.

Jonathan offers the excuse they have planned, explaining that David has returned home to Bethlehem to celebrate the festival and begs the king's indulgence. Jonathan explains that David has observed the correct protocol and that he, as the royal prince, has granted him leave of absence.

Saul accuses his son of treachery. Furious, he picks up his ever-ready spear and hurls it at his own son. Jonathan leaves the palace deeply troubled at his father's reaction, recognising that now life can never be the same again.

The next morning, Jonathan activates the second part of the plan and goes out shooting. He fires his arrows beyond his young servant and gives David the pre-arranged signal. His life is in danger and he cannot return to the palace.

Jonathan sends the young lad back with his weapons and, once the coast is clear, he and David embrace each other. It is a tearful meeting: they both realise that their friendship, however strong, will never be the same again. David is about to embark on the most difficult period of his life. He will now live as a fugitive, on the run from a mad king, until the time is right in God's timetable for him to take the throne.

When that happens, both Saul and Jonathan will be dead.

● *Episode 2 – True friendship has a long memory*

Jumping ahead several years in the David story, we read of a touching incident in his life that recalls the special contract made between him and his friend Jonathan.[9] In the aftermath of the death of Saul and Jonathan on Mount Gilboah, the nation is shocked and grieved. The Philistines have killed Saul and three of his sons. When the news reaches the palace, many of the royal household flee for safety, fearing either a coup or an all-out assault from the victorious Philistines.

Jonathan has a young son called Mephibosheth who is about five years old. The boy's nanny picks him up and runs for safety but in the general stampede she loses her footing and falls. The boy is hurt, suffering fractures that are never properly treated. As a result he remains permanently crippled in both feet. That is a personal tragedy – but he is also socially isolated, disqualified from ascending to the throne. His disability – quite literally – dis-ables him.

Mephibosheth goes into hiding far away. Some years later, David makes enquiries to see if there is any survivor of the royal family he can show kindness to for the sake of his dear friend Jonathan. Hearing the sad story of Mephibosheth, he sends for him. No doubt with great fear, Mephibosheth comes to meet David and bows low to the ground in homage. This could easily have been a plot to flush out any of Saul's family in order to have them executed and stifle any opposition. Mephibosheth takes the lowest place on the floor and asks King David, 'What is your servant that you should notice a dead dog like me?'[10]

But instead of revenge, Mephibosheth finds himself kissed by grace. David tells him of the deep friendship that he and his father Jonathan have shared. To honour Jonathan's memory, David orders that all the property of King Saul should be restored to Mephibosheth and that he should have a place at the king's table and eat there daily. David assigns some of those who were trusted servants of Saul to look after Mephibosheth's interests and to see he lacks nothing. Instantly, Mephibosheth moves from being a refugee to being an honoured son of the king.

These two episodes reveal something of the extraordinary depth of friendship that grows between David and Jonathan. Everything should have made them enemies – but God makes them friends. And the strength of their relationship has spoken throughout the centuries.

Learning from the story

As we seek to learn lessons from this key element in David's life we need to address the question: could David and Jonathan's relationship be regarded as homosexual in any way? There are those who argue the case for acceptance of homosexual relationships on the same grounds as hetero-sexual ones, by claiming that David and Jonathan are a powerful biblical example that God can both initiate and be pleased with same sex partnerships.

Without doubt, the story does speak about the depth of same sex friendships and we can draw some valid conclusions about relationships. But to argue that David and Jonathan were engaged in homo-erotic activity is quite simply a misuse of the text. Scripture is silent and does not need us to fill in the gaps with our own cultural bias. As Professor John Goldingay has expressed it:

> The question has been raised whether the relationship of Jonathan and David was a homosexual one. If that means, 'Did they have sex?' then the story neither says they did nor says they did not, nor does it offer pointers in either direction, so that the question is a pointless one. The story's significance in the context of contempo-rary same-sex relationships surely lies rather in pointing to possi-bilities and raising questions for men to think about as we look at our relationships with other men.[11]

It is always dangerous to read things into the silences of Scripture. But what the story of David and Jonathan does achieve is the recognition that men can enjoy deep friend-ships. It speaks into our contemporary world and has much to teach us about friendship. We know that relationships can do damage. People who claim to be friends can betray us. Some friendships are downright unhealthy, based upon manipulation and control. People can often be trapped in such relationships, unable to change for years. If you have walked away from an abusive relationship, you know you'll limp for the rest of your life.

But over and against this, David and Jonathan's story paints a better picture. Recall the two episodes recorded in Scripture:

- True friendship has strong shoulders
- True friendship has a long memory

With those episodes in mind, think about the quality of the friendship David and Jonathan shared and use it as a ruler to measure your own relational skills.

- Commitment
- Putting others first
- Risk
- Acts of kindness
- Protection
- Thinking and speaking well of another
- Long-term investment
- Loving people when they are absent as much as when they are present
- Not being afraid to show true feelings

There is an echo here of some words from one of the most famous chapters of the Bible, 1 Corinthians 13:

> Love is patient, love is kind. It does not envy, it does not boast, it is not proud. It is not rude, it is not self-seeking, it is not easily angered, it keeps no record of wrongs. Love does not delight in evil but rejoices with the truth. It always protects, always trusts, always hopes, always perseveres.[12]

Such quality of relationships can only come about through the work of God's Holy Spirit in our hearts, for love – real love – is the harvest of the seed only he sows.[13]

There is one other episode in the David and Jonathan story that throws an interesting light on their friendship. The Bible records their final meeting during the dark days when David is running as a fugitive from Saul. At great personal risk, the two of them arrange a clandestine appointment in a place called Horesh. This is what the Bible reveals about their final meeting on earth: 'Saul's son Jonathan went to David at Horesh and helped him to find strength in God.'[14]

In the moment of deepest need, David finds strength in God through the encouragement of a friend. David had the God-given gift of writing words and music that have inspired faith throughout generations. But he knew what it was to be made strong through the friendship of another.

Within the experience of following Christ, there is both need and space for such friendships that inspire, strengthen and encourage. It would be easy to read the story of David and Jonathan and feel a stirring of desire to find a friendship of such extravagant quality. But perhaps we are looking through the telescope the wrong way. It is not so much a case of what I might have but more a case of what I might be.

As Alan Redpath expressed it: 'When I think of that story, my heart is stirred by a desire not only that I might have a Jonathan in my life – that is surely very wonderful, but very selfish – but also that I might find a David somewhere to whom I could be a Jonathan.'[15]

Those words remind us that what we are towards others should be our prime concern. Perhaps there is someone to whom you could be a Jonathan? This story shows us that God is committed to relationships and that we need not fear or avoid them. But, by his grace, we can work hard to make them special.

---

[1] 1 Samuel 18:2, 5.

[2] 1 Samuel 14:1-16 tells of Jonathan and his armour bearer showing incredible bravery in taking on a large group of Philistine soldiers.

[3] 1 Samuel 20:30-34.

[4] 1 Samuel 18:4.

[5] 1 Samuel 18:3.

[6] 1 Samuel 20:12-17.

[7] 1 Samuel 19:1-10.

[8] This whole episode is recorded in detail in 1 Samuel 20:1-42.

[9] The story of Mephibosheth is recorded in 2 Samuel 4:4 and 9:1ff.

[10] 2 Samuel 9:8.

[11] John Goldingay, *Men Behaving Badly* (Carlisle; Paternoster Press, 2000), p150.

[12] 1 Corinthians 13:4-7.

[13] Galatians 5:22-24.

[14] 1 Samuel 23:16. Significantly, Jonathan acknowledges that David will one day be king (v17).

[15] Redpath, *The Making of A Man of God*, p43.

5

Persecuted

Listening to the story – 1 Samuel 19:1-24

G.K. Chesterton said, 'Jesus promised his disciples three things – that they would be completely fearless, absurdly happy and in constant trouble.'

Many take comfort from David's story when facing testing and trials. Although called and anointed, David finds the pathway to the throne anything but easy. Saul is a powerful man and for years does all he can to capture and kill David. This picture of a saint on the run has given hope to those who, through the centuries, have found themselves persecuted for their beliefs.

This particular chapter shows Saul as the persecutor, David as the one persecuted and three people – Jonathan, Michal and Samuel – as peacemakers. We shall consider them in turn.

Saul – the persecutor

Saul is determined to kill David and makes at least six attempts on his life.[1] This antagonism is based on a complex mix of emotions including fear, jealousy and anger. There appears to be a spiritual element as well: the writer describes Saul's dark mood as coming from 'an evil spirit'.[2]

One of the most disturbing elements of this obsessive hatred of David is the way in which it escalates. Saul's hatred is never dealt with – and goes from bad to worse. Having thrown a spear at David twice in an outburst of temper, Saul tries a more subtle approach by offering his eldest daughter Merab in marriage. The condition attached appears to be that David should fight against the Philistines – something which, Saul hopes, will rid him of his rival.[3] But Saul reneges on the arrangement, which publicly humiliates David.[4]

Saul then discovers (no doubt to his chagrin) that his daughter Michal has fallen for this handsome superstar. Saul decides to turn this to his advantage, possibly hoping that he can manipulate her and so render David ineffective as his rival.[5] He sets a grotesque bride price, which David exceeds by killing double the number of Philistines required and dumping their severed foreskins in a sack.[6]

Saul's frustration mounts when he realises two things: first, love is strong and his daughter can't be manipulated as easily as he thinks. She really loves David and Saul can't get between them. Secondly, he sees (yet again) that the Lord's hand is on David and no amount of military might can alter that. Saul holds the office but not the power. So he remains David's sworn enemy.[7]

Jonathan defends his friend David, leading to a peaceful interlude, but another spear-hurling incident ends it. Eventually a death squad is dispatched to David's house. When they are fooled into thinking David is sick in bed, Saul insists he be dragged to the palace where he will kill his rival with his own hands.[8]

David escapes, sheltering with Samuel, who runs a prophets' school in Ramah which appears to have been a place dripping with spiritual power.[9] Here Saul is challenged yet remained unchanged.

Why is Saul so intent on hounding David to death? Why does he calm down (and presumably apologise) and then become consumed with murder once more? I believe Saul is threatened by what he see in David. Eugene Petersen expresses it bluntly: 'Saul hated David because David was good.'[10] I would want to take it a step further. Saul hates David because in him he sees what he could have been yet had failed to be. David's goodness is a reminder of all that Saul has lost.

David – the persecuted

It is worth considering what David could do, given such uncomfortable circumstances.

- He could plot to kill Saul and take the throne by force, arguing that God has chosen him and he is simply 'fulfilling the Lord's will for his life'.
- He could give up, returning home to Bethlehem. By sticking to sheep-rearing he would remove himself both from Saul's sight and his sights.

Instead we see a totally different response. Several things stand out about David during this difficult time:

Integrity

Jonathan supplies a character reference for David that speaks for itself.[11] He praises David's loyalty and courage and affirms he has lived honourably – why should Saul, the king, oppose such a faithful subject?

Grace

A temporary lull in hostilities is the fruit of Jonathan's diplomatic skills. Soon the Philistines attack again. David shows great grace in taking up his post as a military commander and fighting against the enemy invasion.[12] To march under the standard of the man who has tried to kill you takes an enormous amount of grace and good will – David seems to have large reservoirs of both.

Wisdom

When it is obvious that Saul has not changed, David sensibly removes himself from the line of fire. Quickly.[13] By so doing, he reminds us of the importance of good timing. Wisdom tells him sticking around will cause greater problems because his life is at risk. It is interesting to note other instances in the Bible of those who found wisdom to know when to flee and when to fight.[14]

Faith

What is going on in David's private thoughts at this time of personal crisis? Amazingly, we have preserved for us an entry from his personal prayer diary. We can read it three thousand years on. Psalm 59 carries this superscription: 'When Saul had sent men to watch David's house in order to kill him.'

The staggering thing is that David is caught up with worship in a time of crisis, as the psalm concludes:

> But I will sing of your strength,
> in the morning I will sing of your love;
> for you are my fortress,
> my refuge in times of trouble.
> O, my Strength, I sing praise to you.[15]

David is content to commit his way to God and leave his enemies for him to deal with. You discover the quality of a person's faith when the wind blows cold.[16] David passes the test with flying colours.

Jonathan, Michal and Samuel – the peacemakers

It must be hard for Saul that two of his children love David, his sworn enemy. This says much about David and his influence and also about Saul and his lack of it.

You can tell who your friends are in a crisis. David finds his support comes from God, through human hands:

- Jonathan, his friend, gives him a reference
- Michal, his wife, gives him cover
- Samuel, his mentor, gives him a shelter

Jonathan speaks well of David to his father Saul and his mediation has some temporary effect.[17] Jonathan defends David against his own interests, so great is his love for his friend.[18]

Michal warns David of the impending attack on his life and aids his escape under cover of night. She then makes an elaborate attempt to pretend David is ill in bed, unable to get up.[19] When eventually her father discovers her part in the escape plan, she lies to protect her own safety, underlining the risk she has taken.

Samuel has vanished from the public picture at this point. But David seeks him out at Ramah and they take shelter in Naioth. It is significant that David is able to tell Samuel the whole sorry tale and no doubt to receive his wise counsel. The Scripture does not tell us specifically, but we can infer from David's subsequent behaviour that Samuel advises him to hold fast and wait for the Lord's timing. David's anointing, carried out by Samuel many years before, still holds good. He will accede to the throne at God's right moment.

Three friends offer David what he needs in a time of deep crisis. In their own way they seek to bring peace and we are reminded of the words of Jesus in the world's most famous sermon: 'Blessed are the peacemakers for they will be called sons of God.'[20]

Learning from the story

As we reflect on the three elements drawn from this sad episode, we need to bring our own lives under the spotlight.

The persecutor

We may not have allowed jealousy to reach the raging proportions Saul achieved but we are all guilty at times of treating people with less fairness than they deserve.

- We make hasty judgements
- We infer wrong motives

- We put people down and push them to one side
- We withhold good things from them
- We feel prejudiced towards them

The lesson of Saul's life is to allow God to deal with bitterness, jealousy and anger and to find forgiveness and freedom through repentance. His story is desperately sad, as he was never free of his negative feelings towards David. There is another Saul in the Bible who was also a persecutor. But Saul of Tarsus met the risen Lord Jesus Christ on the road to Damascus and underwent a dramatic conversion. He was changed by the powerful grace of God and ended up preaching the faith that he had once tried to destroy.[21]

The Old Testament Saul was consumed with jealousy and never found grace to change. Thankfully, the New Testament Saul did, and his life leaves a simple message: there is hope for us all!

The persecuted

It is not a comfortable feeling, but all who follow Christ seriously sometimes experience a certain sense of stigma. Sometimes it can be viciously obvious and at others insidiously hidden. Either way – it hurts. Eugene Petersen has expressed it:

> We're criticised, teased, avoided, attacked, shot at, abandoned, stoned, cursed, hunted down, snubbed, stabbed in the back, treated like a doormat, and damned with faint praise. Not all of those things, and not all the time, but enough of them and often enough to realise that not everyone shares God's excellent attitude toward us.[22]

We are told that this is normal Kingdom living[23] and we should not be surprised when it rears its ugly head. David's response provides a stunning example of what it means to grow in faith and not be distracted under fire. If we find ourselves pursued at present, perhaps Psalm 59 provides a starting point for our prayers? We are reminded we are also part of a world-wide family called the Church. Today life may be relatively easy for us and we enjoy the benefits of freedom. But many other family members wake this morning, finding themselves in a labour camp, or facing another day in an interrogation cell. Some are unsure if they will survive. Some have not seen their families for so long they struggle to remember them. And all this for the sake of Jesus. In our privileged state we are called to pray for them. 'Remember those in prison as if you were their fellow prisoners, and those who are ill-treated as if you yourselves were suffering.'[24]

The peacemakers

Being made to play piggy-in-the-middle is not much fun unless you are six and in a playground. For adults, it's not a game. Jonathan, Michal and Samuel remind us that non-involvement is not an option if we take Jesus' teaching seriously. Speaking up for people, acting as a mediator, offering shelter and protection, being a listening ear and godly counsellor or challenging injustice are all good things. Some of us need to be encouraged and affirmed in that role – especially when we get shot at from both sides.

Others need to realise that getting involved doesn't make you an interfering busybody. Peacemakers have a vital role to play, not just in international relations but in everyday relationships as well. Peacemaking is a risky and often thankless task. We can be misunderstood and criticised by people we respect. But it is a job that needs doing and brings its own unique rewards. This episode raises some important issues:

- A prejudiced persecutor
- Someone on the receiving end of an unjust attack
- A peacemaker doing their best to pour oil on troubled waters

Which of the three categories fits me best today? And what am I going to learn from David's story?

¹ 1 Samuel chapters 18-20 supply details of Saul's threats to David's life. Three times he threw a spear at David, twice he lured him to attack the Philistines by offering his daughters as 'prizes' and then he sent a hit squad to his home. When all these fail, Saul tried to kill the man he saw as the primary threat to his throne.

² 1 Samuel 19:9.

³ 1 Samuel 18:17.

⁴ 1 Samuel 18:19. It has been argued that David had already qualified to marry Merab by his defeat of Goliath (1 Samuel 17:25).

⁵ See 1 Samuel 18:20ff. The fact that Saul's mind worked in this way reveals two things: the depth of enmity he felt towards David and the depraved state of his heart that he could use his daughter in such a callous fashion. He was not fit to be a father, let alone a king.

⁶ 1 Samuel 18:26-27.

⁷ This is the stark conclusion of 1 Samuel 18:28-29.

⁸ 1 Samuel 19:1ff.

⁹ Reading 1 Samuel 19:18ff it is difficult to reach any other conclusion. Not only do the prophets prophesy but Saul's men are overwhelmed by the presence of the Spirit of God at Naioth. Saul himself has a mighty spiritual encounter when he goes to find David. This was not the first time Saul had known an ecstatic experience of the Lord (1 Sam. 10:1-13). We may puzzle over the precise meaning of this but one thing is very clear. Spiritual experiences, however profound, can still leave a person unchanged. The path to a righteous life may be helped by powerful spiritual experiences but they can never be a substitute for working out the practicalities of holy living in the cold light of day. Saul was so overwhelmed he was laid out for a day and a night on the floor – but when he got up he still hated David with a vengeance.

¹⁰ Petersen, *Leap Over A Wall*, p48.

¹¹ Jonathan speaks up before his father Saul on David's behalf and we read his eloquent tribute in 1 Samuel 19:4-5.

¹² 1 Samuel 19:8.

¹³ 1 Samuel 19:10, 18.

¹⁴ For example, Joseph saved his integrity by sprinting (Gen. 39:11-12) and Paul lived to fight another day by following some wise advice to flee (Acts 9:23-25).

[15] Psalm 59:16-17.

[16] President John F. Kennedy said, 'Only when the winds of adversity blow can you tell whether an individual or a country has steadfastness.'

[17] 1 Samuel 19:4ff.

[18] 1 Samuel 20:17.

[19] 1 Samuel 19:11ff. It seems bizarre that the killers were turned away on the grounds that David is ill. ('I'm sorry but you can't kill him today as he is running a temperature. Could you call back tomorrow perhaps?') But it has been suggested that they were affirming some accepted code of honour that decreed a defenceless sick man could not be touched. If this is so, Saul was not bothered by such niceties and insisted David be carried to him in his bed!

[20] Taken from the opening section of Jesus' Sermon on the Mount (Matthew 5:9).

[21] See Paul's own testimony in Galatians 1:23-24.

[22] Petersen, *Leap Over A Wall*, p48.

[23] See what part hardship training played in early discipleship classes in Acts 14:22 and Revelation 1:9.

[24] Hebrews 13:3.

6

Protected

Listening to the story – 1 Samuel 21:1-15

David is on the run from the fierce anger of King Saul. This is
no passing rage that will soon be forgotten. Saul's paranoia
has reached a new level. It has become a national issue. It is
now public policy that David should be hunted down and
killed. His life is in extreme danger.

We are told of God's protective care towards David at this
difficult time. David himself does not come out well but the
Bible never hides weakness and we are encouraged that our
humanity is mirrored in the lives of its heroes and heroines.

How does David's faith show up in such inhospitable circumstances? One of David's best-loved psalms shows what he
believes when his faith is under fire[1] – or what he comes to
believe when his faith is tested. Some lines particularly stand
out:

Even though I walk
through the valley of the shadow of death,
I will fear no evil,
for you are with me,
your rod and your staff they comfort me.
You prepare a table before me
in the presence of my enemies.

You anoint my head with oil,
my cup overflows.[2]

We read these words in comparative security, admiring their
poetry, but for David this is a real testimony of personal experience. He has lived through the fire – and survived.

This chapter offers two episodes that flesh out the truth of
what David testifies to concerning God's protection. As we
consider what God did for David – let's remember what the
Lord can do for us.

Episode 1 – A friendly priest who thinks David is worthy

David decides the safest place to hide from Saul is somewhere
small and remote. He chooses Nob, just north of Jerusalem on
Mount Scopus. Mainly inhabited by priests, the town is the
site of the Tabernacle. Ahimelech is the senior priest there and
he is both honoured and curious at David's arrival.

He is honoured because David's fame is well known. But
Ahimelech is puzzled – men of David's rank rarely travel
alone. Why has he come? The more he thinks of this, the more
afraid he becomes.[3] The rumours about Saul's jealous rages
against David have no doubt leaked from the palace. There is
speculation about Saul's future as king. Now suddenly – without any announcement – David arrives in Nob without
luggage, weapons or food and not a soldier in sight. What is
happening?

David convinces Ahimelech that Saul has sent him on a top-
secret mission, so confidential that he travels alone – his men
will meet him elsewhere. Ahimelech, convinced by this, is
ready to help.

David has two pressing needs – food and a weapon. The
priest has two difficulties: the only bread available is the consecrated bread that can be eaten only by the priests.[4] Because
of the special circumstances of David's mission, Ahimelech is
willing to let him take the bread as long as the men are
ceremonially clean. On receiving David's assurance about this,
Ahimelech hands over these special loaves.

David's mission for the king is clandestine and he has left the palace without even his sword. But Nob is a priestly town and those who live there do not carry weapons. The only weapon Ahimelech can get is Goliath's sword, held in the Tabernacle as a trophy. It is David's trophy and if he wants to borrow it, who could argue?

David is delighted – this weapon is second to none![5] Even though it has meant bending the rules, Ahimelech offers the help needed when it is needed.

Episode 2 – A foreign king who thinks David is crazy

While David is in Nob, he spots someone who recognises him – Doeg, part of the palace staff, Saul's head shepherd.[6] He is probably there for some religious purpose.[7] Concerned that someone so close to the king has seen him, David realises Nob is no longer safe.

Then he makes what at first appears to be a foolish decision, deciding to travel to Gath, one of the principle Philistine towns. Although there are constant skirmishes between the Israelis and the Philistines, this appears to have been a calm period. Despite the temporary truce, it is reckless of David to travel there. He has killed many Philistines[8] and marches into town carrying Goliath's sword – Goliath from Gath.[9]

What is going on in David's mind? Is this an example of stunning courage, arriving in Gath alone? Or is he being so hard-driven by fear that rational thinking deserts him? Probably David is desperate. He knows Saul is hunting him and the last place he will look is enemy territory.

David probably goes to Gath to lie low but is recognised, placed under arrest and taken before the Philistine king – Achish. His servants tell him of David's arrival and warn about the risk of harbouring such a dangerous opponent.[10] Referring to David as 'the king of the land'[11], they quote the ballad that praises David's warrior skills. It is unlikely that they know of David's secret anointing as king. Most likely they are using the word 'king' to describe his popularity among the Israeli nation.

When David faces Achish he is afraid.[12] Will his gamble pay off? Maybe it is reckless to travel to the heart of Philistine territory. Desperate times call for desperate measures, and David begins to fake a severe nervous breakdown. He dribbles and scratches at the doorway, mumbling and shouting to himself, looking wild-eyed. Achish loses patience and tells his advisers to throw him out. This man is no threat – he is completely crazy. Gath has enough madmen already![13]

David's bold gamble appears to have worked. His life is preserved, not because of his own ingenuity, but because the hand that protects him is the hand of the Lord.[14]

Learning from the story

David's behaviour here is not the best example of living for God – but it is a realistic description of how many of us handle (or mishandle) pressure. The honesty of the story offers us hope and help. As Eugene Petersen warns,

> …the story of David isn't set before us as a moral model to copy. David isn't a person whose actions we're inspired to imitate. In the company of David we don't feel inadequate because we know we could never do it that well. Just the opposite – in the company of David we find someone who does it as badly as, or worse than, we do, but who in the process doesn't quit, doesn't withdraw from God. David's isn't an ideal life but an actual life. We imaginatively enter the company of David not to improve our morals but to deepen our sense of human reality: this is what happens in the grand enterprise of being human.[15]

At this low point in his life, God is at work on David. His route to the throne is difficult but necessary because he is being trained to lead. Alan Redpath captures this succinctly: '…what is happening to David at this point is all in the will of God to make of him a man of God. It takes but a moment to make a convert; it takes a lifetime to manufacture a saint'.[16]

There are a number of lessons within this chapter of David's life from which we can learn, particularly about fear, faith, flexibility and faithfulness.

A lesson about fear

Fear leads us to do silly things. We fail to think straight, react in panic, thinking and behaving irrationally. This is precisely what happens to David. When he arrived at Nob and talked with Ahimelech, he lied. When he thought he had been spotted, he fled to Gath and, when discovered, he was afraid again.[17] This led to his pantomime performance to convince Achish that he is mad and therefore harmless.

Before we sit in judgement on David, we need to reflect on our own fear reactions which at times lead us to lie or act in strange ways. Perhaps we need to learn from David's story that faith and obedience are better options to follow.

A lesson about faith

Fear is part of being human. It is what we do with our fear that counts. Faith is the great antidote to fear, which is why we need to learn how to feed it. For as someone once said, 'When you feed your faith you starve your doubts to death.'[18] David wrote a couple of psalms at this difficult stage of his life. In one of them (Psalm 56) he openly confessed his fear and how he found God's help at the lowest point:

When I am afraid, I will trust in you.
In God, whose word I praise,
In God I trust; I will not be afraid.
What can mortal man do to me?[19]

You can sense the steely determination that lies behind these words – 'I will' and 'I will not' have an emphatic edge to them. We understand from the superscription that this was written when he had been arrested in Gath. Perhaps he was in custody waiting to stand before the king? Or maybe this was after he pretended to be mad and was thrown out of the palace? Either way, we have a glimpse into David's heart and discover it is quite like our own. His personal testimony of strength received gives us strength to fight our own battles with fear:

> I am under vows to you, O God.
> I will present my thank-offerings to you.
> For you have delivered me from death
> and my feet from stumbling,
> that I may walk before God
> in the light of life.[20]

A lesson about flexibility

We switch the spotlight for a moment from David to Ahimelech, a brave and honourable man. The reason we focus on what I call his flexibility is because the Lord Jesus referred to him.[21] Jesus and his disciples were under fire from the religious leaders for contravening accepted practice for observing the Sabbath. Jesus' followers were picking heads of grain and eating them, which was defined as work by the Pharisees, and roundly condemned. Jesus dismissed their criticism with a stinging rebuke. He quoted the incident of David being given the consecrated bread to eat and cited this as an example of God's flexibility on such matters. The Pharisees had utterly missed the point. The Sabbath was made for man, not man for the Sabbath. Ahimelech's behaviour, according to Jesus, was close to God's heart because mercy is preferable to sacrifice.[22]

This does not mean we are free to be flexible with God's moral laws and to practise what some have called situation ethics. But it does challenge us to be flexible where matters of tradition and culture are concerned. Perhaps, like the Pharisees, we can elevate things far higher than God ever intends and end up majoring on minors. Many splits in churches and between friends could have been avoided if the Ahimelech approach had been adopted.

A lesson about faithfulness

As mentioned before, David wrote two psalms at this dark time in his life. The second was Psalm 34 and the superscription reveals it was written: 'When he pretended to be insane before Abimelech, who drove him away and he left.'[23] David reflected on all that took place and this psalm reveals his view of God's faithfulness. He was fully aware that this episode had not brought out the best in him but he had been an unworthy (yet grateful) recipient of the grace of God in his life.

You might find it helpful to find a quiet place and read through this psalm, which was painstakingly composed to help others find faith in God.[24] It is full of God and stands as an eloquent testimony to his faithfulness. Many of its phrases are familiar quotes:

> Taste and see that the Lord is good ... The angel of the Lord encamps around those who fear him ... I sought the Lord and he answered me and delivered me from all my fears.[25]

The most outstanding thing about this period in David's life is the faithfulness of David's God. Even though David scored two out of ten for handling a crisis, God gets a ten. And David merely mirrors our own experience. We take heart in the overwhelming grace of our great God. Because of his outrageous grace, we find strength for a new day because, 'The Lord redeems his servants; no-one will be condemned who takes refuge in him.'[26]

---

[1] Psalm 23, sometimes referred to as 'the Shepherd's Song', gives an eloquent description of the life of faith lived under the sovereign protection of the Lord as Shepherd.

[2] Psalm 23:4-5.

[3] 1 Samuel 21:1 – Ahimelech trembled when he met David.

[4] Leviticus 24:5-9 – there were twelve loaves baked weekly and replaced each Sabbath. The loaves are sometimes called 'the bread of the presence' or showbread.

⁵ Goliath was a giant of a man and his weaponry and armour were legendary. See 1 Samuel 17:4-7.

⁶ Some argue that Doeg's job was head of the palace guard and as such his presence at Nob was doubly dangerous for David. See Petersen, *Leap Over A Wall*, p65.

⁷ Doeg was an Edomite and it has been suggested he may have been converted to Judaism and his presence at Nob was connected with this.

⁸ 1 Samuel 18:27, 30. David was known and feared by the Philistines.

⁹ 1 Samuel 17:4.

¹⁰ It is probable that David slipped into Gath discreetly and his presence was spotted by others. He was then summoned to Achish to explain why he was there and pretended to have lost his mind. What threat could a madman be to the king of Gath?

¹¹ 1 Samuel 21:11.

¹² The Bible is very honest about David's state of mind: 'David took these words to heart and was very much afraid of Achish' (1 Sam. 21:12).

¹³ One explanation for this strange incident is that David hid in Gath and was put on trial before King Achish. David seemed insane – within the criminal justice system today he could be classified 'Unfit to Plead'. A mad runaway was no threat. Possibly the killing of someone thus disabled was regarded as dishonourable – even making those who attacked him liable to a curse on themselves. (See page 44 endnote 19).

¹⁴ David is under no illusions about what brought him through this tough experience. Both Psalms 34 and 56 reflect his feelings that God was his sovereign protector.

¹⁵ Petersen, *Leap Over A Wall*, p62.

¹⁶ Redpath, *The Making of A Man of God*, p68.

¹⁷ 1 Samuel 21:12.

¹⁸ David's decision to flee to Nob may have been prompted by a deep desire to find God at this turbulent time. On a previous occasion he had sought out Samuel for counsel and support (see 1 Samuel 19:18ff) and it may have been too dangerous and obvious to return. But Nob, which housed the Tabernacle, may have drawn David towards the spiritual refreshment he craved.

From 22:15 we understand that David had asked Ahimelech to enquire of God for him and this would support the view that he was looking for the Lord at this tough time.

[19] Psalm 56:3-4.

[20] Psalm 56:12-13.

[21] The incident is recorded in all three of the Synoptic Gospels – Matthew 12:1-8, Mark 2:23-28 and Luke 6:1-11.

[22] This quote from Hosea 6:6 echoes a prophetic note of the Old Testament, that it is possible to pursue the letter of the law yet miss the spirit of it.

[23] Abimelech (not to be confused with Ahimelech!) was the dynastic title of the royal line to which Achish belonged. See Genesis 26:1 for the start of this dynasty of Philistine kings where the original Abimelech meets Isaac.

[24] Psalm 34 is an acrostic with a clever use of letters of the alphabet – suggesting that considerable thought had been given to its composition.

[25] Psalm 34:8, 7, 4.

[26] Psalm 34:22.

7

Fugitive

Listening to the story – 1 Samuel 22:1-23

David is not a man to back away from a fight and the shame of having to play-act complete vulnerability demoralises him. There is more than a hint of a new resolve in David's heart as he moves on from Gath.[1] Leaving the city, he finds refuge in a cave close to a city, just over the border between Philistia and Israel. His family secretly join him. Saul threatens them too and there is always the dreadful possibility that they could be held hostage in order to flush David out of hiding.

Word spreads about the fugitive family hiding in the cave of Adullam. Soon others join this refugee camp. The writer of the Bible narrative describes David's new extended family: 'All those who were in distress or in debt or discontented gathered round him, and he became their leader. About four hundred men were with him.'[2]

The anointing of God is on David to lead the nation – even though the time is not yet right. But the anointing of God has no need of title, position or human permission. David begins to lead – and others follow that lead – because God called him to be a leader.

Desperately concerned about the welfare of his family, David decides to hide them safely. He has family ties in Moab, on the far side of the Dead Sea well away from Saul's clutches.

David knows they will be safe and negotiates with the king of Moab for his parents and family to live there temporarily.[3] His comment to the king of Moab reveals his heart: 'Would you let my father and mother come and stay with you until I learn what God will do for me?'[4]

David is evidently moving on in his understanding of God. While in Moab, he receives a prophetic word of warning from a man by the name of Gad. He urges David not to go back to the cave but to Judah and he makes his new camp in a forest.[5]

Word reaches Saul of David's whereabouts and he holds court on what to do next. In these intervening weeks, Saul's paranoia has increased.[6] He accuses his closest advisers and officials of plotting against him. Saul believes there is a double conspiracy at work: that Jonathan is plotting with David to overthrow his own father and these close royal officials are keeping quiet about it.[7]

Doeg, Saul's head shepherd, hears what is going on with the royal advisory team.[8] He tells Saul how Ahimelech the priest has helped David.[9] Saul, his suspicions further fuelled, sends for Ahimelech and his whole family. Saul accuses him of conspiring with David in an act of treason, by offering sanctuary, food, weapons and spiritual guidance to this public enemy. Ahimelech is scared and confused. As far as he is concerned, David is Saul's loyal subject, the king's son-in-law, captain of the bodyguard and a highly respected member of the royal household. Ahimelech agrees he helped David – he has done so frequently and cannot understand what has changed. If David is caught up with any plot against the king, Ahimelech knows nothing about it.[10]

Saul is convinced of Ahimelech's guilt. He orders the chief priest and his family to be executed immediately. But the royal guards are too afraid to strike down the one anointed by God as spiritual leader of the nation. Their fear of Saul is great – but their fear of God is greater. Saul commands Doeg to carry out the dreadful deed and he does so. Here is a chance to get a place of power. Not only does Doeg kill Ahimelech, but eighty-five priests as well. In a fit of blood-lust he travels to

Nob, annihilating every living creature within it – men, women, children and animals.[11]

One of Ahimelech's sons – Abiathar – escapes the carnage. He reaches David and tells the horrific story of the murder of Yahweh's servants and their families. David is grief-stricken – recognising his own responsibility for what has happened.[12] But he is quick to offer shelter to this traumatised man, showing once again that he is a leader, not because it is in his job description but because it is part of his character. His words to the bereaved Abiathar are evidence of a shepherd heart: 'Stay with me; don't be afraid; the man who is seeking your life is seeking mine also. You will be safe with me.'[13]

Learning from the story

There are five characters who play significant parts in this episode of David's story and their actions are noteworthy for very different reasons:

- Saul
- Doeg
- Ahimelech
- Abiathar
- David

Saul – a man who was sinking

Saul had lost touch with God and his life began steadily to unravel. Raymond Brown describes it this way:

> When a man or woman becomes indifferent to the voice of God, tragic things can happen. Selfish desires and the casual sayings or criticisms of friends will assume a far greater importance than they deserve. It was so with Saul. Had he been in touch with God, the success of David would have encouraged him. He would have rejoiced that, at a critical time in the nation's life, a valiant man had

been raised up by God to lead His people to freedom from the Philistine oppression.[14]

Sin is very sociable. There were a clutch of sins apparent in Saul: self-pity as he condemned his closest courtiers, saying that no-one cared about him; outright suspicion of others' motives and intentions; uncontrolled anger as Saul denounced Ahimelech and accused him of treason; injustice as he judged Ahimelech, assuming he was guilty even before he defended himself; and murder, as he ordered the execution of Ahimelech and his fellow priests. Saul was also implicated in the awful slaughter of every living creature at the town of Nob.[15]

Saul's life reminds us of the crucial importance of keeping close to Jesus. Saul had known the word of God selecting him to be king, he had received the anointing of God for this important task, he had benefited from the close mentoring and encouragement of Samuel. Saul had received so much. But he lost it because he rejected God. The awful events of this chapter are the fruits of that rejection.

As Jesus taught in the words of the Parable of the Sower, it is one thing to receive the word of God but quite another to act upon it: 'The seed on good soil stands for those with a noble and good heart, who hear the word, retain it, and by persevering produce a crop ... Therefore consider carefully how you listen.'[16]

Doeg – a man who was climbing

It would be hard to find a greater example of naked opportunism than Doeg. John Calvin describes him as 'the consummate villain'.[17] He was in charge of the shepherds and a foreigner from Edom.[18] He was prepared to push others out of the way, to be economical with the truth and had no hesitation in obeying Saul's orders to kill Ahimelech and the other priests. In order to secure himself fully in Saul's inner circle he led the slaughter in Nob.

We are stunned by the evil of this man. And we are reminded that ambition is like fire. It can warm but it can also burn. David, on learning the news of Doeg's treachery, summed him up: 'Surely God will bring you down to everlasting ruin: he will snatch you up and tear you from your tent; he will uproot you from the land of the living.'[19] We are reminded of the power of ambition and the need to submit it to God. Heed the wisdom of Scripture: 'Do nothing out of selfish ambition or vain conceit ...'[20]

Ahimelech – a man who was suffering

Ahimelech was a good man who fell foul of a bad man and reminds us that we live in a world where bad things do happen to good people. The (temporary) triumph of evil and the slaughter of innocents have been part of the human experience since Adam first chose to ignore God. Ahimelech and the godly priests of Nob, together with their families, also remind us of the ultimate triumph of the justice of God.

Whenever injustice occurs and we cry out, 'That's unfair!' we anticipate the day when absolute fairness will triumph. God will have the last word.[21]

Abiathar – a man who was running

Abiathar was Ahimelech's son and seems to have been the sole survivor of this massacre. We do not know how old he was at this time – or how he managed to escape. But we do know two important things about him. Firstly, David's invitation must have presented a challenge to Abiathar. David (or at least Saul's jealousy towards David) was the cause of the problem and he was partly responsible for the death of Abiathar's family. David's assurance of security could have rung hollow. But Abiathar trusted him. We also know he stayed with David, becoming a senior priest and trusted adviser at court.[22] He grew from personal tragedy to be useful to God – an encouragement to any who feel they have been overtaken with grief to such an extent they will never be used by God. His is a story of hope for all who want to rebuild a shattered life.

He became part of that 'Adullam Team' that David assembled, people with a wide variety of needs who all found hope and security in him. Preachers of previous generations have indulged in something known as typology. This involves reading into Old Testament Scriptures New Testament truths. It is a precarious process and sometimes does violence to the text but there are occasions when the Bible illustrates itself – and this is an example.

David gathered around him what one writer describes as 'a motley group'.[23] That is a picture of what Jesus has done in gathering his people – the redeemed of God – pending his full coronation as King. The prince of this world is on his throne but Jesus is anointed, approved of God and will reign one day. We are his 'Adullam Team' and we are reminded how this assorted band grew to be such skilful and brave warriors.[24]

We are also reminded that following Christ is not simply about finding security – true and great though that is. We are also called to learn and grow and to move from a place of distress and discontent to a position of fruitfulness and fulfilment.

David – a man who was growing

David was a different man from the one who fled to Nob and pleaded with Ahimelech for help. God was answering his prayers and the evidence is seen by the fruit in his life. As Saul's disobedience brought bad fruit so David's obedience produces good fruit.

We know that David wrote several psalms at this time of living as a fugitive.[25] They make it clear that his gaze was fixed on God. Whatever help might come his way, David knew the Lord was the source,

I cry out to God Most High,
  to God, who fulfils his purpose for me.
He sends from heaven and saves me, rebuking those who hotly
  pursue me;
God sends his love and faithfulness.[26]

The fruit of this growing faith is seen in several instances in this episode. Taking his parents to the safety of Moab tells us much about his state of mind, not least the request to the king of that country, 'Would you let my father and mother come and stay with you until I learn what God will do for me?' [27] David was providing for his family, but not with any overconfident self-reliance. He was watching the overarching purpose of God, that he could see being worked out before his eyes.

We can also see growth in David as a person, with his ability to face responsibility in his frank admission to Abiathar. David takes on himself some responsibility for the murders at Nob – but this is not a self-pitying kind of admission. David shouldered his responsibility by offering shelter to Abiathar, revealing the maturity of his admission.[28]

This chapter also reveals the growth of David as a leader. Others gathered around him, looking to him for direction.[29] His anointing was apparent to others. David was not king because of a title, a throne and a large army. These are Saul's symbols of power – although his grasp was shaky. God's call and anointing marked David out unmistakably. And others noticed.

The challenge David brings to us is the challenge to grow.
And let the hard times make us strong.

---

[1] Careful study of Psalm 56, written after the events in Gath reveals a man who has come to a new place of confidence in God. Twice he asks the question 'What can man do to me?' as if this has dominated him for a time. The strong note echoing through the psalm is confidence in God who has delivered him from death.

[2] 1 Samuel 22:2.

[3] This is not as strange an arrangement as it may seem to a modern Western mindset. Family ties were strong in David's day – and remain so in many non-Western cultures today. David's family ties were strong in Moab. His great grandmother Ruth came from there (Ruth 1:4 and 4:21-22).

[4] 1 Samuel 22:3.

[5] 1 Samuel 22:5 – Saul may have been given information about the stronghold David had established at the cave of Adullam – it would be difficult to keep that number of people and livestock a secret. But God protects David by steering him away from danger.

It is significant that, in response to David's statement that he wants to know what God has in mind for him, the Lord speaks through an unknown prophet in a foreign place.

6 One tell-tale phrase is worth noting here. We are told that Saul sat with his officials 'spear in hand' (1 Sam. 22:6). His subsequent verbal assault on his most loyal advisers shows how deeply suspicious and insecure he has become. Saul probably didn't sleep well – if at all. He believed the whole world was out to get him.

7 Palace plots were not unknown – even close family members would kill relatives in order to seize power. But Saul's fears are groundless. His closest associates were family members from his own tribe of Benjamin (1 Sam. 22:7) and they knew their economic livelihood was linked to Saul's continuance on the throne. Jonathan was steadfastly loyal to his father to the end – and died alongside him in battle.

8 Doeg was unlikely to be taking part in these high-level talks – he was primarily concerned with livestock. Maybe Saul had (another) angry outburst and the deliberations of this privy council spilled out to other royal officials. Doeg seized an opportunity for self-advancement that had not offered itself before.

9 1 Samuel 21:7.

10 Ahimelech (thinking quickly on his feet) realises his suspicions about David's secretive arrivals at Nob were well founded. His main line of defence was he acted in good faith, ignorant of anything David was involved in that could be construed as trea-sonable (1 Sam. 21:1-2).

11 We are not told that Saul specifically ordered Doeg to take this action. But even without Saul's direct order it is most unlikely that he could have done this dreadful thing without his approval. Such a wholesale slaughter would have taken a large group of armed soldiers.

12 1 Samuel 22:22. In what way did David feel responsible? His decision to flee to Nob (where Doeg recognised him) contributed to these murders. At a deeper level, he may have realised that his decision to deceive Ahimelech (rather than take him into his confidence) placed him in a more vulnerable position, Either way, David showed great maturity by owning up to responsibility and being committed to facing the consequences.

13   1 Samuel 22:23.

14   Raymond Brown, *Skilful Hands – Studies in the Life of David* (London; Lakeland, 1972) p58.

15   See 1 Samuel 22:6-19.

16   Luke 8:15, 18.

17   Cited by Petersen, *Leap Over A Wall*, p 67, quoting from *John Calvin, Commentary on the Psalms* (Vol 2) (Grand Rapids: Eerdmans, 1949) p311.

18   1 Samuel 21:7.

19   Psalm 52:5: David wrote this when he heard the news of Doeg's betrayal of Ahimelech.

20   Philippians 2:2.

21   Revelation 20:11-15.

22   1 Chronicles 15:11.

23   Redpath, *The Making of A Man of God*, p77ff.

24   1 Chronicles 12:8 describes their bravery and skill.

25   See superscriptions for Psalms 34, 52, 57, 142.

26   Psalm 57:2-3.

27   1 Samuel 22:3.

28   1 Samuel 22:22-23.

29   1 Samuel 22:2.

8

Leader

Listening to the story – 1 Samuel 23:1-29

Asked to define leadership, one leader replied, 'There are only three kinds of people in the world – those who are movable, those who are immovable, and those who move them.'[1] The art of successful leadership is knowing *how* to move people. This episode from David's life reveals that, because he was led, he knew how to lead.

David and his growing band of men are living in hiding in the forest of Hereth[2] when a message reaches them that the Philistines are attacking. There is a border town named Keilah several miles from where David and his men are based. It is harvest season and the people are bringing in the crops and processing the grain. When the hard work is complete, groups of armed Philistines come across the border to take the processed grain. There are casualties as the people of Keilah try to defend their livelihood.

David chooses to get involved – but not as a knee-jerk re-action: 'he enquired of the Lord'.[3] Receiving a positive response, he musters his men. Reluctantly, they point out, reasonably, that they are living as fugitives from Saul, daily facing betrayal and capture. Tense and afraid, getting involved in someone else's battle will not help – and could make things worse. Their message? 'Don't get involved.'

Here is a leader faced with the immovable. What does he do? Exerts his authority, stamps his foot, changes his mind or negotiates a compromise? 'Once again David enquired of the Lord, and the Lord answered him.'[4] When his authority is challenged, David returns to the source of his authority. Once more he receives a clear word of instruction and the assurance that he will defeat the Philistines under God's power.

Armed with this, David persuades his men and they help the people of Keilah. Inflicting heavy losses on the Philistines, they take their livestock in compensation. The one who should have helped the people of Keilah is Saul, but his obsession with finding David is absorbing all his energies and those of his army. He has abandoned his responsibilities as king.[5]

The narrator offers some insight as to how David found his guidance from God at this important time: 'Abiathar, son of Ahimelech, had brought the ephod down with him when he fled to David at Keilah.'[6] Having escaped the mass slaughter at Nob, Abiathar has managed to bring with him his father's ephod. This is a garment worn by all priests, but a special one belonged to the High Priest.[7] Added to this robe are other items such as a turban and breastplate.[8] Contained within the breastplate are two stones known as Urim and Thummim, used when seeking guidance from the Lord on a particular matter.[9] Moses had instructed that these be used as the primary method of discovering God's will in any matter.[10]

There is a deep significance in Abiathar's action in rescuing the ephod and bringing it with him as he sought refuge with David. Saul has displayed total contempt for the Lord in his murder of Ahimelech and the total annihilation of the priests of Israel and their families, which has cut him off from the God of Israel. The ephod, the symbol of priesthood and all that meant, has been rescued and taken now to David. The Urim and Thummim – symbols of Yahweh's leadership and direction of his people – has passed to David. The writer of this record is signalling transfer. Saul's kingship is on an irreversible slide as David's is ascending.

Saul views religion as a commodity. David, in his earliest days with the Urim and Thummim, demonstrates a deeper view. He seeks God and his success as a leader is bound up with his capacity to be led.

Treachery is a dreadful thing – even worse when it comes from the hands of those who owe a debt of gratitude. David's feeling of triumph over the raiding Philistines turns sour when Saul learns of his success, and that David and his men are enjoying the hospitality of the people of Keilah. He realises that David is potentially trapped inside a town with gates and walls, easy to pin down and kill.[11]

But David's confidence isn't in the thickness of the walls that surround him nor in the strength of his forces. Sending again for Abiathar and the high priest's ephod,[12] David spreads the rumours of Saul's impending attack before the Lord and asks two vital questions:

- Will Saul come to Keilah?
- Will the people of Keilah betray David?

The answers he receives from the Urim and Thummim are difficult – Saul will attack and the town's leaders will betray. So David and his men, now numbering around six hundred,[13] escape and keep moving on to shake Saul off. And Saul constantly keeps fruitlessly searching – 'But God did not give David into his hands.'[14]

Even in this period of great uncertainty, nothing happens to David through chance. God's protective hand spans his life. David is ultimately secure. He is even able to meet Jonathan. Saul can't find David, yet Jonathan appears to have no difficulty doing so.[15] This is a poignant meeting, the last time the two friends meet on earth. Jonathan 'helped him to find strength in God.'[16] This is a profoundly spiritual experience and David comes away with his faith renewed. Jonathan makes God bigger and Saul smaller and David treasures that adjustment to his perspective. David hears the will of Yahweh reaffirmed and this enables him to move forward in faith.[17]

But he remains vulnerable. The people of the region of Ziph, where David has been hiding, prove as treacherous as the people of Keilah, offering Saul help to catch David.[18] Saul gratefully encourages them to gather as much intelligence as they can about David's location, particularly details of his various hiding places. Saul knows David's skill at escaping.[19]

As the net closes in, Saul and his men are summoned. Alerted, David moves south to the desert of Maon.[20] Saul comes even closer: the two groups are on different sides of the same mountain. Then, at the vital moment, a messenger appears with an urgent message for Saul. The Philistines have invaded: Saul and his troops are urgently required elsewhere.[21]

At the last minute, David and his exhausted men are saved. Yahweh has sheltered David and, once more, preserved his life.[22] David and his men made camp at En Gedi, an oasis close to the shores of the Dead Sea.[23]

Learning from the story

At this point of his life, David is undergoing major reconstruction. Through his straitened circumstances God is shaping him, building the principles of kingship into his life. What is going on is largely hidden – but one day would be revealed. In this period, there are several interlinked strands from which we can draw wisdom.

The value of the wilderness

Wildernesses are, by definition, wild places, unkempt and unspoilt. David began to spend time in the wilderness at this point, first in the desert of Maon and then at En Gedi, which led into the most barren, wild landscape, full of high rocks and caves. David's wilderness years began here and would encompass fifteen significant life episodes.

The Bible often refers to wilderness periods: the nation of Israel spent forty years wandering through one. The Lord Jesus spent forty days and nights of temptation in the wilderness and Paul found his foundational training there.[24]

God uses the wilderness to train, refine and reveal. Eugene Petersen refers to the 'circumstantial wilderness' where we are no longer in control and find the familiar removed. He maintains: 'I readily acknowledge that this circumstantial wilderness is a terrible, frightening, and dangerous place; but I also believe that it's a place of beauty. There are things to be seen, heard, and experienced in this wilderness that can be seen, heard and experienced nowhere else.'[25]

The wilderness can be a growing place. We should see it as an opportunity to grow deeper and wider in our relationship with God and others.

The importance of seeking God

David asked God for direction in his life, an earnest seeking for God's mind and purpose. When challenged by his own men, David went back to the source of his guidance. When threatened by Saul, David looked to God for the answer to his questions.[26] There is no better test of an individual's spirituality than how they go about making decisions. The person with a heart for God will always seek his will in all things – both large and small.

The strength of true friendship

This final meeting between David and Jonathan is a wonderful reminder of how friendship can make a vital difference in our lives. None of us is an island. We need companionship to prosper. Sadly, our Western culture has elevated individualism at the expense of a proper understanding of community. David's story reminds us of the richness of true friendship. Jonathan expressed a depth of love and partnership with David that is a true testimony to the grace of God. His friendship strengthened David's grasp of God. May our friendships be as productive.

The first principle of leadership

The first principle of leadership is often forgotten. It is, simply, if you are going to lead, you must first be led. There is an incident from Jesus' life that illustrates this. A Roman officer sent a message to Jesus asking him to help one of the man's servants who was desperately ill. Jesus set off to the officer's home but before he arrived, he received another message. The Roman officer asked Jesus not to visit because he did not feel worthy to have Jesus even enter his hallway. Instead, he asked Jesus to say the word of command, knowing his servant would be healed. The officer commented: 'For I myself am a man under authority, with soldiers under me. I tell this one, "Go", and he goes; and that one, "Come", and he comes. I say to my servant, "Do this", and he does it.'[27]

Jesus was stunned by such a grasp of faith and used this anonymous Roman as an example, commenting that he had not found a Jew with such a level of faith. It had taken a foreign gentile to reveal such a great capacity for belief.

But the puzzling thing about the incident is the Roman's assertion that he was a man under authority. We would expect him to say, 'I am a man with authority, so when I issue a command it is carried out.' But instead he illustrates the first principle of leadership – if you are going to lead, you must first be led. He was under the authority of those above him. That gave him the power to lead others. He saw this same principle at work in Jesus. As the Son of God, Jesus was working under the authority of the Father. That is why he could say the word and the sick servant would get better.

A major work of construction was underway in David. God was building a king who would be a man after his own heart. One of the valuable lessons David learned was to look to God as the source of his strength, for therein lies true authority. He learned the lesson well, for as one of the psalms he wrote at this time reveals, David knew where his authority lay: 'Surely God is my help; the Lord is the one who sustains me.'[28]

---

[1] This quotation comes from Li Hong-Zhang, the nineteenth-century Chinese statesman, who responded to a question about the nature of true leadership put by General Charles Gordon.

[2] 1 Samuel 22:5 – they had gone there directed by God through a prophetic word.

3 1 Samuel 23:2.

4 1 Samuel 23:4.

5 It is worth noting that David held true to his anointing, already acting as a king even though he is yet to be crowned. Already he is a better king than Saul.

6 1 Samuel 23:6.

7 1 Samuel 22:18 reveals that all the priests wore the linen ephod. Exodus 39:1-31 gives details of the High Priest's ephod.

8 Exodus 28:1-43.

9 Moses' instructions are quite explicit on this point. These are no mere lots to be cast with superstition – there is a deep sense of God's guiding presence at work within the process; 'Also put the Urim and the Thummim in the breastpiece, so they may be over Aaron's heart whenever he enters the presence of the Lord. Thus Aaron will always bear the means of making decisions for the Israelites over his heart before the Lord' (Ex. 28:30).

10 Numbers 27:21. The Urim and Thummim seemed to decline in influence as the role of the prophets took on greater importance. How the stones worked is still a matter for discussion.

11 1 Samuel 23:7-8. Inside a town with gates and walls David had created a siege situation where Saul would hope either the people of Keilah would hand him over or he could take the town by his superior military strength.

12 It is interesting to note that Abiathar is referred to (for the first time) as 'the priest' (1 Sam. 23:9). Up until now he has been described as the son of Ahimelech (see 1 Sam. 22:20, 23:6). This raises a question; was Abiathar already a priest when his father was killed (or at least a priest in training)? Or did the slaughter at Nob lead to David making a fast-track appointment of the son of the murdered High Priest to his father's post?

13 The numbers seem important to the writer. At the cave of Adullam, the group numbered four hundred (1 Sam. 22:2) but now the number had risen to six hundred, an increase of a third. This increase seems to indicate David's growing influence and military strength.

14 1 Samuel 23:14.

15 David longed to see Jonathan and, quite literally, trusted his friend with his life. He probably sent word to Jonathan about

where they could meet. The two took an enormous risk in so doing.

[16] 1 Samuel 23:16.

[17] 1 Samuel 23:16-18. Two things stand out from Jonathan's words of encouragement. (1) Saul knew in his heart that David would replace him as king – and it was obvious to all that knew him that this was so. (2) Jonathan believed he would be around when David made it to the throne and would gladly take the second place. He was wrong as he died in battle before David's accession. But it reveals much about his humble and willing spirit that he could contemplate such a thing. It would be unthinkable for this to happen. A change of dynasty was rarely bloodless and the heir apparent gladly making way for another non-family member would be beyond comprehension.

[18] 1 Samuel 23:19. The Ziphites' behaviour perhaps reflects the extent of Saul's power. Just as the people of Keilah were potentially threatened into betraying David, so the Ziphites may have concluded their long-term interests were better served by co-operating with the ruling power.

[19] 1 Samuel 23:21-23. David had escaped several times and Saul wanted plenty of information before embarking on the manhunt again.

[20] 1 Samuel 23:24-25. This was a wilderness area close to a city called Maon.

[21] 1 Samuel 23:26-28.

[22] For the Bible's dramatic account of this momentous event in Israel's history see Exodus 14:23-31.

[23] 1 Samuel 23:29. The use of the word 'strongholds' suggests that David either made or made use of fortifications.

[24] Luke 4:1-13 has the wilderness temptations of Jesus and Galatians 1:17 has Paul's account of his early years as a follower of Christ in the desert.

[25] Petersen, *Leap Over A Wall*, p74.

[26] 1 Samuel 23:2, 4, 9ff.

[27] Luke 7:1-10.

[28] Psalm 54:4 which was written when David heard the Ziphites had agreed with Saul to track him down.

9

Follower

Listening to the story – 1 Samuel 24:1-22

David and his six hundred men are living in the desert of En Gedi, hiding from Saul, skulking in caves, careful to conceal their whereabouts. Saul is still determined to catch David,[1] and he has learned David and his men are in a specific area in the desert of En Gedi called the Crags of the Wild Goats. Gathering a force of three thousand men, Saul again sets off in pursuit of David.[2] But this time Saul falls into David's hands.

Saul answers a call of nature and, seeking privacy, goes into a large cave. David and his men (or possibly some of them) are hiding in the back of the cave, out of sight. The mad monarch, usually heavily armed and closely guarded, is alone, vulnerable. David's men whisper their urgent encouragement:

'The Lord is good – he has answered your prayers. He is keeping his promise to you that you would take the throne. Your destiny lies in your hands – *seize it!*'[3]

David creeps slowly towards Saul, keeping close to the cave wall. A host of possibilities tumbles through his mind. If he slits Saul's throat, there is still an army outside the cave to deal with. Perhaps they can be persuaded to accept David as king. He knows he has Jonathan's blessing. Can this be a bloodless coup – except for the blood of Saul? The world will be a better place without him. Fear will vanish, the running can stop.

David and his men can go home to their families and farms. They can hug their wives and kids for the first time in months, sleep in their own beds ... and the throne God has promised him will be David's. All of this is seconds away if David will steel himself to attack an unarmed man.

David decides not to use his sword to tear Saul's skin but to cut a strip of cloth from his royal robe. He quietly makes his way to the back of the cave to rejoin his men as Saul finishes what he has come to do and goes out to meet his army.

David's men are mystified and indignant. Why has he passed up such a chance? Some want to grab Saul before he left the cave – if David doesn't have what it takes, then they certainly do! David stops them and confesses his feelings of overwhelming guilt.[4] His men can't believe what they are hearing. David is confessing his sin of presumption rather than his failure to seize the moment!

But David is convicted about his action in reaching out his hand against the one God has placed as king over Israel. Saul has been anointed for this task.[5] This anointing is the tangible sign of his appointing – the Lord's doing. The moment Saul ceases to be king is down to God – not David. His grief and repentance come to his heart because he sees how close he has come to seeking to manipulate the will of Yahweh. One of the many lessons about kingship David has been learning is that the Lord is the ultimate ruler. His will must prevail above all. In order to lead you must first be led.[6]

David makes a bold decision, going out into the daylight. Saul and his men are further down the valley when shouts reach them. Saul turns and can't believe his eyes (or his luck) for there is the unmistakable figure of David.

But he isn't hurling threats. He is kneeling low in the dust, going through the respectful motions that any king can expect from his loyal subject. David says in measured tones:

'Your majesty – don't listen to those advisers who tell you I am out to kill you. If that is true, then why didn't I take your life a few minutes ago? Some of my men urged me to do it – and think me crazy for ignoring them. But I told them – you are the king Yahweh has anointed and I dare not lift my hand against you. Your majesty – my father – look at what I have hidden in my hand! It is a corner of your royal robe that you removed when you came into the cave. This is how close I came. I chose to spare you. Judge my actions. Is this how a man bent on treason behaves? If I am out to take your life – why did I spare you? If I am the greatest threat to your reign – then why did I choose to let you alone?

Let the Lord judge between us who is right and wrong – I have no intention of getting my own back. As the old proverb says, "Bad people do bad things". But see from this good thing I have done in sparing your life – that I am a good man. You are the king of Israel – and what am I by comparison? A dead dog – or a flea? I give my case to the Lord. May he decide between us and prove me right by delivering me from your hand.' [7]

Saul's men fix their gaze on the king, awaiting his order. How will he respond to David waving a piece of the royal robe in his hands?

Saul is silent for a long time as he stares up at David. Then his shoulders begin to shake and the tears course down his cheeks. His voice cracking with emotion, he shouts,

'David my son? Is it really you? You're a better man than me, for you have treated me well whilst I have treated you so badly. I believe you when you say you can be trusted. I fell into your hands yet you spared my life. This is how a friend behaves, not an enemy. May the Lord bless you for your treatment of me this day. I believe you will be king one day – God will bring it about and the kingdom will grow under your hands. Only promise me when this happens you will be kind to my family and deal well with them.' [8]

The fighting men who witness this strange encounter cannot believe their eyes or their ears. Saul's men have been dragged across a vast wilderness on a manhunt in pursuit of David and now they see their target being allowed to slip away.[9] Saul, who has been breathing out venom against this most dangerous man, is now weeping and calling him his son. Few of them can make any sense of this strange state of affairs.

David's ragged bunch of fighters has come to admire his leadership skills. But many of them believe he has made a fatal mistake when he has the chance to rid himself of Saul. His enemy is in his hands and he has let him go. How many leaders have fallen because they lacked the 'killer instinct'? Then he has broken cover and put all their lives at risk. His speech, which is about as grovelling as you can get, when he declares himself to be Saul's friend, has left them mystified.

David solemnly promises that Saul's family will be safe in his hands – after all, he has proved his faithfulness this very day. The two groups separate. Saul and his men go back to the palace and David and his fighters back into their camp in the desert of En Gedi.[10]

Learning from the story

Each of the fifteen stories linked to David's wilderness years is a progress report on God's training programme, equipping David to become Israel's king. We may never be called to the task of running a nation, but as followers of Christ; other, no less weighty responsibilities beckon. David's lessons can become our lessons too as we seek to be people after God's own heart.[11] We learn about

- Reverence
- Respect
- Right choices

Reverence

David's wilderness period has been an opportunity to discover more about himself and, most of all, about his God. Eugene Petersen says about this period:

...as David was dealing with God, a sense of the sacred developed in him. While he was living in that austere country, his awareness of holiness, of God's beauty and presence in everything, in everyone, increased exponentially. David was above all reverent. He had an inordinate capacity for wonder. The Psalms, many of which came out of these wilderness years, are our main evidence for this.[12]

When we are away from the public gaze, the true measure of our faith is seen. David had the opportunity to kill Saul and seize the throne for himself. What held him in check was not cowardice (as most of his men believed) but reverence. David made that abundantly clear by his conscience-stricken declaration of regret that he had cut off part of the king's robe.[13]

The Bible says, 'The fear of the Lord is the beginning of wisdom.'[14] David demonstrated what this means by his decision not to harm Saul out of reverence for God. What we believe should affect the way we behave. In David's case it undoubtedly did.

Respect

It is difficult to understand this concept of deep reverence for the king, especially for a bad one. David could have done himself and the nation a great favour by killing Saul. But he had respect for the man's office. Saul was the king appointed by the Lord and, until Yahweh decreed otherwise, he was due the respect owed to a king.

No less a responsibility is placed on the shoulders of all who follow Jesus Christ. Peter, the first-century Christian leader, wrote these surprising words; 'Show proper respect to everyone. Love the brotherhood of believers, fear God, honour the King.'[15] They are surprising because they were written at a time in history when 'the king' was the Roman emperor. Some of the emperors promoted outright persecution of Christians. Peter himself was probably martyred under the authority of the infamous Nero. Yet this sense of respect is encouraged – why? The answer is that the governing authorities are God-ordained to preserve order, unity and safety within society.[16] So we are encouraged both to offer respect and to encourage others to do the same.

But David also had respect for Saul as a person. David didn't hear Jesus preach the Sermon on the Mount. But he got the message. Jesus said, 'You have heard that it was said, "Love your neighbour and hate your enemy." But I tell you: Love your enemies and pray for those who persecute you, that you may be sons of your Father in heaven.'[17]

Few of us will ever know (thank God) what it means to face an enemy who seeks our life. We will not live as fugitives on the run from someone totally obsessed with eliminating us. But, sadly, we will find people who will see and treat us as their enemies. This Old Testament story illustrates a New Testament truth. Bitterness, unforgiveness, resentment and the pursuit of revenge are out if we want to follow Jesus well.

Right choices

Choosing is an important part of life, from big decisions to mundane matters. We know it is possible to choose well and also to make mistakes. It is important to note that David chose to ignore advice from those close to him at this critical point. His men urged him to see Saul falling into his hands as a God-incidence. But David steadfastly refused to give way. In fact, he was convicted about his decision to cut off a corner of the king's robe.[18] David made the right choice because he was learning to keep his eyes and ears open to the Lord.[19]

---

[1] Petersen uses a powerful little phrase to convey Saul's total obsession with killing David; 'Saul was running after David, obsessed with hunting him down, his life narrowed to a murderous squint.' Petersen, *Leap Over A Wall*, p80.

[2] Saul came close to David at Selah Hammahlekoth (1 Sam. 23:26-29) and knew the strength of his force (six hundred men). He selects an army over three times that size.

[3] 1 Samuel 24:4. See NIV margin – another way of translating this verse is 'Today the Lord is saying to you …' – suggesting there

was perhaps an element of prophecy surrounding their urging. David's men want him to see this as an opportunity from the hand of the Lord.

4   1 Samuel 24:5-6.

5   1 Samuel 10:1ff has details of Saul's appointment. This included Samuel pouring oil over his head and announcing that Yahweh had anointed him as ruler of his people. Saul's job description was clear – he was a steward called by God and entrusted with the task of leading the Lord's people.

6   David's words make for careful study and reflection. He refers to Saul as 'my master', 'the Lord's anointed' and 'the anointed of the Lord' in one sentence (1 Sam. 24:6).

7   1 Samuel 24:8-15. David's impassioned speech is a model in diplomacy. He makes his case well but does it in a way designed to calm Saul rather than provoke him further.

8   1 Samuel 24:16-22.

9   It is probable that these men were involved in the intense manhunt detailed in 1 Samuel 23:25ff and were then redeployed to repel the Philistine invasion. Fresh from this conflict they resumed their search for David in the uncomfortable terrain of the En Gedi desert. This was a long and arduous tour of duty and they now had to cope with the object of their strategy being allowed to slip through the net.

10   1 Samuel 24:2.2

11   1 Samuel 13:14, 16:7.

12   Petersen, *Leap Over A Wall*, p77.

13   1 Samuel 24:5-6.

14   Proverbs 9:10.

15   1 Peter 2:17.

16   Romans 13:1-5 gives an apostolic explanation of how authority is ordained by God.

17   Matthew 5:43-45.

18   1 Samuel 24:5.

19   Psalm 142.

Controlled

Listening to the story – 1 Samuel 25:1-44

A sad day dawns in Israel when Samuel dies. This man has been a loyal servant of Yahweh for many years and has given spiritual leadership to the nation through difficult times. The Bible tells us that the whole nation mourns his passing.[1]

An interlude occurs in the saga of the ongoing tensions between Saul and God's chosen replacement as king – David. It is marked by an episode in which David is prevented from carrying out a murder and ends up by marrying a wife.

David and his growing army move to an area eight miles south of Hebron known as the desert of Maon.[2] A wealthy landowner is introduced into the story – Nabal. He owns land and animals and is well known in the local community, as is his wife, Abigail. But they are famous for different reasons. Abigail is known as a beautiful intelligent woman. Nabal is known for being surly and tight-fisted.[3]

It is the season of the year for sheep-shearing, which is also a time for feasting. David sends a group of his men to Nabal with a courteous request, consistent with the contemporary culture of hospitality. David is asking for some food in recognition for the protection offered by his men towards Nabal's herds over the preceding months.[4] It is a well-intentioned request – but it falls on deaf ears. Nabal's response is rude. Refusing David any food, he insults him: 'Who is this David? Who is this son of Jesse? Many servants are breaking away from their masters these days. Why should I take my bread and water and the meat I have slaughtered for my shearers, and give it to men coming from who knows where?'[5]

David's men return empty-handed and repeat Nabal's rude reply. David is furious at such a gross insult, and orders his men to arm themselves. Taking four hundred with him, he leaves the rest on guard. He is going to avenge himself.[6]

Meanwhile, Nabal's closest servants have heard what their boss said to David's men. Having probably learned the hard way that Nabal isn't open to having his decisions questioned,[7] they know his wife is ready to listen to reason.

The servants explain what has happened – how Nabal has sent David's messengers away empty-handed, in spite of the integrity with which David's men have acted in protecting Nabal's property and herds. The servants can see what their master fails to recognise – his response has brought the threat of disaster upon the whole household.

Fortunately Abigail lives up to her reputation as a woman of outstanding intelligence. She immediately issues some detailed instructions about food, but decides wisely not to tell Nabal what she is doing.

David and his men are approaching when Abigail appears.[8] She quickly bows low to the ground at David's feet,[9] pleading with David to show mercy, in spite of her husband's gross insult.[10] In summary, she makes the following points with great eloquence:

- Any blame for the incident should be placed at her door
- Her husband is a fool by name and nature[11]
- If David's servants had gone to Abigail they would have received a different answer
- Her substantial gift of food should be received as a peace-offering
- Yahweh had stayed David's hand from vengeance
- David would one day become king over Israel

- When that day arrived, David would not want the blood-shed of Nabal and his men to spoil his conscience
- David is the Lord's man and no-one (not even a fool like Nabal) can rob him of that rich inheritance

David is deeply affected by what he hears. In a matter of min-utes his heart changes and he acknowledges that Abigail is a messenger of the Lord to him.[12] David receives her gifts with grace, acknowledging her wise words have changed his mind. David returns with his men, his honour satisfied, and Abigail goes home to face Nabal. She left without telling her husband what she intended to do – but her actions will not remain a secret. She needs to tell Nabal what she has done – but that moment needs to be chosen with great care.

At home, she finds Nabal drunk beyond reason, so she wisely decides to put off the awkward confrontation until morning.[13] Then Abigail tells Nabal of her intervention with David. Nabal – either from shock or anger – suffers what appears to be a severe stroke from which he never recovers.[14] Scripture says; 'About ten days later the Lord struck Nabal and he died.'[15]

This story has a happy ending that hints at why the incident was first recorded. Abigail makes a big impression on David and he recognises the hand of God in their meeting. He sends for her with a proposal of marriage, which she gladly accepts. Abigail becomes David's second wife alongside Ahinoam from Jezreel. The writer of 1 Samuel points out that David's wife, Michal (Saul's daughter), has been taken and given to another man.[16] This was another action on Saul's part to humiliate David.

Couples often meet in curious circumstances – perhaps few more strange than the meeting of David and Abigail. David's heart is moved from murder to marriage in the space of a few days.[17]

Learning from the story

There are three principal characters in this story and lessons can be learned from each of them.

- Nabal – a foolish man
- Abigail – a beautiful woman
- David – a teachable servant

Nabal – a foolish man

Nabal was aptly named because he lived like a fool. The description given of him in Scripture is as unflattering as any you will find. One writer of another era suggested when Jesus painted with words the parable of the rich fool, Nabal sat as model for the portrait![18] He is surely the one of whom it was originally said, 'The lights are on – but no-one is home.' He was a man who had great wealth and no doubt great influence to go with it. But he had no character and there lay his weakness.[19] The Bible story shows up his weakness in so many areas;

- His lack of wisdom
- His lack of respect
- His lack of honour
- His lack of understanding
- His lack of self-discipline
- His lack of love
- His lack of courtesy
- His lack of awareness
- His lack of humility

Perhaps the saddest thing was the statement made by one of his closest aides: 'He is such a wicked man that no-one can talk to him.'[20] Those closest to us know us best. This anonymous servant summed up what all who worked with Nabal knew to be true. You couldn't tell him anything. There were only two opinions on any subject – Nabal's and the wrong one. Before closing your mind to this unsavoury character, join me in praying a simple but heartfelt prayer, 'Lord, the older I get, make me more teachable and willing to learn.'

Abigail – a beautiful woman

One of the immediate questions on reading this story is, how did a woman like this end up married to a man like that? But Abigail and Nabal are not the first instance of an unlikely alliance. In an era of arranged marriages, it would be highly likely that Abigail had had little say in the choice of a husband. She might have been married as a teenager to a man many years older than herself. Her story is an encouragement to those trapped in difficult marriages with partners who leave a lot to be desired.

The writer is keen to bring out the contrast between Nabal and his wife. His uncouth nature was offset by Abigail's beauty and wisdom. But as her speech to David shows, she possessed a beauty that was more than skin deep. There was a radiance of character that shone through her actions and words.

One curious part of the story is how Abigail moves from being the victim to becoming the heroine. She was trapped in a less than happy marriage and looked like becoming a widow very quickly. But rather than allowing circumstances to dictate to her, Abigail seizes the moment and is used by God to transform the situation. She gives hope to any of us who feel powerless, by showing it is possible – even for those who are marginalised – to make a difference. Abigail made a difference by being willing to act, doing it promptly, employing tact with great skill and seeing the bigger picture of God's overall plan. She changed David's mind – and won his heart.

It would be a huge mistake simply to read this as a case of a pretty woman sweet-talking an angry man. There is depth to her conversation with David that draws him back into fellowship with God. Filled with anger and the desire for revenge, David set out to avenge his name – and lost God in the process. Abigail comes to him as a prophet of the Lord. She reminds David of his high and holy calling and in an inspirational turn of phrase, strikes a chord that reverberates in his heart: 'the life of my master will be bound securely in the bundle of the living by the Lord your God. But the lives of your enemies he will hurl away as from the pocket of a sling.' [21]

Her choice of phrase was truly inspirational. The pocket of the sling was a jolt to David's memory. With a sling and a stone he faced Goliath and won. Abigail reminds David of the principles by which God had set him out on his journey to the throne. He didn't need to sort out Nabal. God could handle it. David simply needed to concentrate on preparing for kingship and refusing all distractions. She reminded him of his destiny.[22]

David – a teachable servant

At this point, David has a respite from his long-term struggles with Saul. The throne is inching nearer, his influence is continuing to grow. These are dangerous moments, when he is perhaps tempted to rely on himself rather than God.

David was angry and many of his contemporaries would see his intentions as justifiable. But the slaughter of Nabal and his men would have left a deep stain on David's career. It would have been political suicide to engage in the slaughter of a well known landowner – however churlish his behaviour. To win the minds and hearts of the people of Judah, David needed to show restraint, not might.

David's strength of character is seen in two ways: first, he was prepared to take advice. Nabal's ears were closed to any opinion but his own: David showed openness. Second, David was willing to take advice from an unlikely source. In his culture, Abigail was 'a mere woman' – her status was low. And she was married to the man who had insulted his honour. But David's teachability meant he would listen to advice from a most unlikely source.

Being prepared to listen and learn is the mark of a mature follower of Christ. One church leader rather memorably described an ideal church as being full of FATSOS. It's an acrostic worth remembering for the wisdom it contains:

Faithful to God, to his word and to the leadership
Available to God in the use of their time and opportunities
Teachable by the leaders, circumstances and the Spirit

Sound in New Testament Christianity, both orthodoxy and
orthopraxy
Outgoing in social skills so as to maximise their impact
Spirit-led in the development of character and obedience to
Jesus.[23]

Nabal, Abigail and David form an unlikely trio – but they offer
lessons on life and how to live it skilfully.

---

[1] 1 Samuel 25:1. Samuel was an influential figure in this difficult
period of Israel's history. He had served the Lord during a time of
enormous change, the last judge in the three hundred and fifty
year span of the Judges period, and was the first of the prophets
(see Acts 3:24), the prime mover in the establishment of the
monarchy in Israel. He did not live to witness David's coronation
but perhaps he knew of Saul's acknowledgement that his throne
would pass to David in accordance with the word of the Lord
through Samuel (see 1 Sam. 24:20).

[2] 1 Samuel 25:1. David's men numbered around six hundred at this
stage (see 1 Sam. 25:13) but allowing for camp followers such as
wives and children, they made up a large company. The constant
need to find provisions for this number explains the approach
David makes to the wealthy Nabal.

[3] The Bible pulls no punches in a very concise summary of Nabal
and Abigail (see 1 Sam. 25:3).

[4] It has been suggested that David employed this as a means of finding food for his camp. His men would offer protection to the herds
and flocks that surrounded them, particularly from raiding parties
from other nations. In return local landowners would offer food
and drink to David by way of payment for services rendered.

[5] 1 Samuel 25:10-11.

[6] By his own admission, David set out with murder in his heart
(1 Sam. 25:21-22).

[7] The servants' comment to Abigail about her husband is most
telling, 'He is such a wicked man that no-one can talk to him'
(1 Sam. 25:17).

[8] Reading 1 Samuel 25:21-22 raises a few difficulties for those familiar with the Sermon on the Mount! There is no love for enemies or

turning the other cheek here. (For Jesus' way of handling enemies, see Mt. 5:38-48.) But the Bible does not seek to justify David's intended actions. He was kept from committing what would have been a terrible sin.

9 To bow low was a sign not only of respect but of servanthood – as David himself had done to show his loyalty to King Saul (1 Sam. 24:8). By such a humble act, Abigail was paving the way for her impassioned plea to be heard.

10 Abigail's speech is a model in diplomacy. It is more than an abject apology and declares God's intention that David would one day be king over Israel. Her appeal for restraint is couched in terms that were difficult for David to ignore. She set the whole incident in the context of the larger purpose of God.

11 The name Nabal means 'fool' in Hebrew.

12 David's immediate response to Abigail's speech is, 'Praise be to the Lord, the God of Israel, who has sent you today to meet me' (1 Sam. 25:32).

13 1 Samuel 25:36 reveals three things about Nabal that further confirm his complete stupidity. (1) He has thrown a lavish banquet 'like that of a king' i.e. completely beyond what was appropriate and over the top. (2) He was in high spirits – oblivious to the fact that his wife was pleading for his life. (3) He was very drunk – at a time when his household was facing annihilation.

14 The description given in 1 Samuel 25:37 suggests a stroke: 'his heart failed him and he became like a stone'.

15 1 Samuel 25:38.

16 1 Samuel 25:44.

17 Marriage to more than one wife was common practice, particularly for men of wealth and social standing. Marriages also brought political benefits. 'Political marriages were common at the time, and by his marriages to Abigail and Ahinoam David was making important links with influential families in Judah. His future way to kingship would be due to the support of the tribe of Judah, not because of any support from the existing royal court. The writer does not say so, but he plainly saw David's marriage to Abigail as part of God's plans for him.' *The New Bible Commentary* (21st Century edition) (Leicester: IVP 1994) p318.

[18] See F.B. Meyer, *David – Shepherd, Psalmist, King* (London: Marshall, Morgan and Scott, 1953 edition) p97.

[19] Meyer, *David – Shepherd, Psalmist, King*, refers to four types of greatness – p97. It is possible to be great in possessions, great in achievements, great in thinking but the fourth 'great' is best of all: to be great in character.

[20] 1 Samuel 25:17.

[21] 1 Samuel 25:29.

[22] Petersen puts it this way, 'Abigail recovers God for David. David is earlier described as beautiful (1 Sam. 16:12; 17:42), though there's no sign of it here. But beautiful Abigail (25:3) restores the beauty of God to David, his original identity.' He points out that in all three scripture references the same Hebrew word for beauty is used: *yaphah*. *Leap Over A Wall*, p82 and corresponding footnote.

[23] John McClure, leader of the International Vineyard Fellowship. *The New Encyclopaedia of Christian Quotations* p600.

11

Darkened

Listening to the story – 1 Samuel 26:1 – 27:12

Most of us are familiar with the process of testing. We accept it as routine and expected. In the realm of spiritual growth, God has his own testing process that evaluates progress.[1] David, still living as a fugitive, now faces a further testing period in God's development programme. The results are mixed. David does well and badly – and reminds us that we may have tasted grace but we live flawed lives as well.[2]

He and his men have returned to an area known as the desert of Ziph. Once again, the unreliable Ziphites give information to Saul about David's location – perhaps in the hope of some reward from the king's hand.[3]

Saul sets off in pursuit of David with a large force of three thousand soldiers. When Saul's army arrive and settle themselves into camp for the night, David's own intelligence service warns him. Surprisingly, he doesn't make use of the cover of darkness to escape and find another bolthole. Instead, he sets off on a night-time reconnaissance mission with two of his most trusted men.

They discover that Saul and his army are asleep.[4] David suggests he should go into the camp – and Abishai volunteers to go too, leaving Ahimelech back at their hiding place.[5]

They creep into the camp, past the sleeping soldiers, to the centre where King Saul and his most trusted commanders lie sleeping. At Saul's head, pinned into the ground, is his own spear with its distinctive markings. Abishai sees this moment as a God-ordained opportunity for David to be rid of his enemy and to replace Saul on the throne. He wants to run the sleeping Saul through on the spot – but David stops him.

Once again, David resists the temptation to speed up God's timetable. His whispered warning to Abishai reveals what controls his motives. 'Don't destroy him! Who can lay a hand on the Lord's anointed and be guiltless? As surely as the Lord lives ... the Lord himself will strike him; either his time will come and he will die, or he will go into battle and perish. But the Lord forbid that I should lay a hand on the Lord's anointed.'[6]

Instead, David takes Saul's spear and water jug and the two men stealthily leave the camp.[7] No-one sees them and, once they are a safe distance away, overlooking the location, David calls out a sarcastic taunt to Abner, Saul's senior commander. 'Abner, where are you? Time to wake up! What about your reputation and that of your brave men? The king should be safe when you're around, shouldn't he? What happened? While you are having a rest someone came and stole something belonging to the king. Can you guess what's missing? Try finding the royal spear and water jug – they look very like the ones I am holding up here, don't they?'

The camp is in chaos – but Saul cuts across the noise with his strong voice:

'Is that your voice, David my son?'[8] David answers with characteristic respect, 'Yes it is, my lord the king.'[9] Then David asks Saul why he is treating him as his enemy, chasing him like a criminal. David sets out the options boldly;

That Saul has been sent by the Lord to punish David

If this is the case, then David promises to make an offering as atonement for whatever sin he may have unwittingly committed.

That Saul has been incited against David by others

If rivals have told Saul lies about David's ambitions and behaviour, then let them be cursed of God. By their actions, they have turned David into an outcast, ruined his life, and are pushing him from his homeland to live abroad and worship foreign gods. David does not want to die in exile – estranged from his homeland and faith. Who is David anyway, compared to Saul and his might? Saul's pursuit of David is like swatting a flea or hunting a bird![10]

Once again, Saul exhibits a quite extraordinary and rapid change of heart. David's act of mercy and restraint has touched him and proved that this is not the action of a man bent on bringing his reign to an end. Saul shouts his candid confession in the presence of his men, 'I will not try to harm you again. Surely I have acted like a fool and have erred greatly.'[11]

David invites Saul to send a man to collect his spear. He calls out what must have been a deeply heartfelt prayer to God, as much as it is a plea to the king, 'As surely as I valued your life today, so may the Lord value my life and deliver me from all trouble.'[12] David's eyes are on the Lord, believing that righteous actions never go unrecognised in his eyes and that he rewards those who seek to live with integrity.

Saul concludes this bizarre meeting[13] with a blessing that has a prophetic ring: 'May you be blessed, my son, David; you will do great things and surely triumph.'[14]

Saul orders his men to withdraw and returns with them to the royal base at Gibeah and David rejoins his men at their desert stronghold.

In part one of this test, David passed with flying colours. But the next episode is not so encouraging. The Bible warns that 'Pride goes before destruction, a haughty spirit before a fall.'[15]

Perhaps David feels a flush of triumph in his decision to let Saul off. As he returns to his men, Ahimelech and Abishai lose no time in passing on the news of David's astonishing bravery. He soars even higher in the opinion of his troops – this latest exploit pushes David along the pathway to becoming a legend in his own lifetime.

At moments of great triumph we are at our most vulnerable.

David faces the second part of his test with an unhealthy and unrealistic assessment of his own abilities. Worse still, he begins to rely on his own insight rather than God's.

This dangerous slide is seen by the way David reasons with himself and ends up living in the land of the Philistines; 'But David thought to himself, "One of these days I will be destroyed by the hand of Saul. The best thing I can do is to escape to the land of the Philistines. Then Saul will give up searching for me anywhere in Israel and I will slip out of his hand."'[16]

David and his men make their way into Philistine territory and go to the main city of Gath where Achish is the king.[17] David's 'family' is sizeable and he needs to negotiate a deal that will enable them to stay in Philistia.[18] Achish agrees with David's suggestion that they make their home in a Philistine city, Ziklag, a long way from Gath, at the southern end of Philistia.[19] The Bible narrator adds the helpful comment that David set a precedent so that ownership of Ziklag passed down to other kings of Judah in succeeding years.[20]

At one level David's plan seems to work. Saul gives up his relentless search[21] and David and his team spend sixteen months in peace and safety.[22]

But their peace is costly.[23] Such a large crowd of people need food and drink and David and his men launch raiding parties against some of the tribal groups that live in the northern part of the Sinai desert. They follow the practice of other nomadic groups, stealing animals and goods. We are told that David and his men decide to take no prisoners. This is a politically expedient move, for two reasons. No survivors mean no reprisals, and they can deceive the Philistines into thinking they are attacking their own nation of Israel. This will create the impression that David has made himself so despicable in the eyes of his fellow Israelites that he will never be able to return to his homeland. To have David and his army as allies is a useful asset to King Achish and one he prizes greatly. So whenever David's raiding parties return with their plunder and are asked where they have attacked, they give false locations in the country of Judah, thus keeping up the appearance that they have turned on their own people.[24]

By resorting to human tactics to provide security, David fails the test of trusting in God alone. This sad episode reveals what is true about all of us. When it comes to the tests that God sets, we can win and we can lose.

Learning from the story

When David fled to Ziklag, he had been living as a fugitive for seven years. He would wait another three years before Saul was killed in battle and the throne passed to him. But at this stage, he had no knowledge of how long he had to wait. It could be another three or thirty years, for all David knew.

Something of the anxious longings he felt are echoed in a psalm:

> How long, O Lord? Will you forget me for ever?
> How long will you hide your face from me?
> How long must I wrestle with my thoughts
> and every day have sorrow in my heart?
> How long will my enemy triumph over me?[25]

When this time of testing came, David was feeling the pressure of impatience. How long until God would fulfil his promise? It is worth comparing the two episodes side by side and contrasting the difference between the tests, the responses and the results.

Test 1 – the power test

Abishai urged David to take charge of his own destiny and offered to kill Saul for his master. David's refusal was based on three important principles:[26]

- God's anointing
- God's timing
- God's purpose

David saw Saul as the anointed king and rejected any notion that he should raise his hand against him. He recognised that God's timing is perfect and that – when it was right – Saul would die and the throne pass to David. But he had no intention of hurrying things along. Thirdly, David's overriding concern was for God's will to be fulfilled and he was content to leave every detail in the Lord's hands.

Test 2 – the patience test

We read David's dialogue with himself and it is an instructive exercise. His reckoning was awry on several fronts:

- His view of Saul
- His view of himself
- His view of God

Saul had become bigger than God. David was convinced that, 'One of these days I will be destroyed by the hand of Saul.'[27] David had been worn down by seven years on the run – and who can blame him for feeling despondent? Perhaps the glow of success from showing mercy to Saul a second time inflated his sense of pride and led to self-reliance. Warren Wiersbe wisely warns,

> God's children must be careful not to yield to despondency. Moses was discouraged over his heavy workload and wanted to die (Numbers 11:15) and Elijah ran from the place of duty because of fear and discouragement (1 Kings 19). When we start to look at God through our circumstances instead of looking at our circumstances through God's eyes, we will lose faith, patience and courage, and the enemy will triumph.[28]

David was dominated too by feelings about himself. The telltale phrase at the start of 1 Samuel 27 says, 'He thought to himself'. Here was the man who had learned from his earliest years to talk to God – now talking to himself. It was a very one-sided conversation. Count the number of times the words 'I' and 'me' occur. David was placing himself at the centre of his thinking rather than God.

David had lost sight of the Lord. Not long before, David had enquired of God before taking major decisions[29] but now it is his own wit that governs his choices.

The outcome of David's failure was plain. He and his men were compromised and engaged in the sort of bloodthirsty border raiding that most of the surrounding tribal warlords lived by. Once again he deceived the Philistine king Achish and, at one level, seemed to prosper. But in terms of his spiritual development this was not a good result.

It would be too easy to sit in judgement on David but that is not our task. If we are honest, his inconsistencies are uncomfortably close to home. They remind us of our own tests, whether in the realms of power, patience or in other complex areas – temptation, relationships, resentment and ambition. To aid us in our own battles, we would do well to learn from David's success and his failure. The difference between the two is seen most clearly by where the control lies; with ourselves or with God.

David wrote the words of Psalm 32 and they throw an interesting light on his experience of the testing work of God,

> I will instruct you and teach you in the way you should go;
> I will counsel you and watch over you.
> Do not be like the horse or the mule, which have no understanding but must be controlled by bit and bridle or they will not come to you.[30]

The horse can be impulsive and ready to charge, the mule stubborn and reluctant. Both need the control of bit, bridle and occasionally a large stick! But the Lord looks for more than a relationship of a master to a dumb animal.

We – like David – have a calling and destiny as children of the King. He wants us to live as such and to look to him for the direction of our lives in accordance with his will.

All the tests we face have one design – to draw us closer to him.

---

1. Jesus used the word picture of a vine being cut back so that it might grow better (Jn. 15:2). This illustration from nature shows us that God allows – sometimes brings – tests in our lives in order that we may grow in faith.

2. Scripture makes no attempt to hide the paradox of people of faith being touched by failure. For example, the story of the call of Abraham (Gen. 12:1ff) reveals his single-minded determination to pursue God's will. He leaves familiar surroundings in obedience to God and travels through the Promised Land building altars, worshipping God and believing an incredible promise. Yet in the same chapter we are told that he passes off his wife as his sister, forcing her into a compromising situation with another man. Abraham travels from faith to fear in the space of a few verses. Reading Scripture is like looking in a mirror (see Jas. 1:22-25).

3. 1 Samuel 23:19ff has the previous incident of betrayal by the Ziphites.

4. Did Saul's men fail to post a guard? Perhaps they felt overconfident that David was more concerned with escape than attack.

5. Before we are tempted to write Ahimelech off as a coward, it is worth considering his role as a lookout. If David and Abishai were spotted and captured, Ahimelech would have the task of coming up with a rescue plan!

6. 1 Samuel 26:9-11.

7. The writer is keen to point out that there was a divine hand at work in David's bold plan. 1 Samuel 26:12 says, 'They were all sleeping because the Lord had put them into a deep sleep.'

8. 1 Samuel 26:17 – there is something pathetic about Saul's recognition of David (see 1 Sam. 24:16-17). David was his son-in-law so he was correct in calling him 'my son' – but it also revealed the enormous internal struggle Saul was undergoing. There was some sense of love for David but it was subsumed by a passionate loathing of him as a rival for the throne. Saul was a deeply troubled man with a cocktail of contradictory emotions pumping through his heart.

⁹ David never lost his respect for Saul's office. His actions were consistent with what he said he believed about Saul.

¹⁰ David's speech to Saul (1 Sam. 26:18-20) shows how desperate he felt about his situation and the fact that he felt he would die in exile; 'Now do not let my blood fall to the ground far from the presence of the Lord' (v20).

¹¹ 1 Samuel 26:21.

¹² 1 Samuel 26:24 – this statement has a psalm-like feel to it (see Ps. 34:6, 142:7).

¹³ This is the last meeting between Saul and David which perhaps adds greater significance to Saul's admission which follows.

¹⁴ 1 Samuel 26:25 – Saul had been given a prophetic gift at the time God had singled him out to be king (see 1 Sam. 10:6-7, 9-13).

¹⁵ Proverbs 16:18.

¹⁶ 1 Samuel 27:1 – David's thinking is ruled by fear. He takes the view that one day Saul will kill him and that God's intention for him to become king will be thwarted.

¹⁷ 1 Samuel 21:10-15.

¹⁸ We are told that David's men numbered six hundred and, in addition, they had wives and children with them (1 Sam. 27:2-3) so it is likely that the camp totalled several thousand.

¹⁹ Ziklag was located twenty-five miles southwest of Gath on the border of Simeon but under Philistine control. The city had associations with the tribes of Simeon and Judah (see Josh. 15:31, 19:5).There was, therefore, a natural reason for Achish to allow David and his men to live there. It was an ideal base, being close to Israel but far enough away from Gath.

²⁰ 1 Samuel 27:6.

²¹ 1 Samuel 27:4 – Saul was put off from pursuing David into enemy territory as this would spark conflict with the Philistines. He called off his surveillance as soon as he was told David and his followers had moved to Gath.

²² 1 Samuel 27:7.

²³ It is worth considering all that Ziklag offered David: safety from Saul, the security of living in a walled city; regular food and drink and a new start for his men and their families. But this came with a price tag. The Philistines were long-standing enemies of Israel; their pagan religion was far removed from worship of Yahweh

and the moral climate vastly different from that which David and his followers had been brought up with. David opted for security but ended up with compromise.

[24] David's deception worked, 'Achish trusted David and said to himself, "He has become so odious to his people, the Israelites, that he will be my servant forever"' (1 Sam. 27:12).

[25] Psalm 13:1-2. But the psalm ends on a note of confident faith that God will act. In his escape to the Philistines David seems to have lost that confidence – or at least temporarily mislaid it.

[26] 1 Samuel 26:9-11.

[27] 1 Samuel 27:1.

[28] Warren W. Wiersbe, *Be Successful – Attaining Wealth that Money Can't Buy* (Victor: Colorado Springs, 2001) p146.

[29] 1 Samuel 23:2, 4, and 9ff. Ironically this was about whether or not to attack the Philistines!

[30] Psalm 32:8, 9.

12

Strengthened

Listening to the story – 1 Samuel 28:1 – 30:10

Compromise can start small yet rapidly increase. David and his men, having chosen to live in Philistine territory, find themselves marching out against their fellow Israelites, under an enemy banner. King Achish has no reservations about their trustworthiness. But his top military commanders do not share his confidence.[1]

Achish has to withstand a serious threat of revolt among his officers, who flatly refuse to allow David and his men to ride with them. King Achish explains his embarrassment to David. Although he has complete confidence in his loyalty, he acknowledges his commanders do not. He asks David not to march against Israel. David feigns deep disappointment – but must be relieved that he is spared the moral dilemma that would have accompanied him and his men into battle.[2]

David and his men return to Ziklag, which is a place of security for them after years of living as fugitives. It is a long way to the south of Philistine territory and it is the third day before they reached home.[3] As they draw near to the city, they sense something is wrong. None of the look-outs are in place. Then they can see plumes of smoke rising into the blue sky. It is the wrong time of day for fires to be lit. There are no signs of life. No women in the fields, no sheep grazing on the riverbank, no children playing around the city gates. Nothing. Ziklag is a ghost town.

The city gates are wide open, unguarded. Some of the men who have ridden ahead report there is no-one in the city. David and his men ride in and begin a thorough search. The city is ruined. Houses burned to the ground, goods looted – rubble and burning timber greet the returning army. Not a soul walks the ruined streets. Everyone and everything has been taken. The place they have come to know as home has been totally trashed.[4]

David and his men weep, loud and long until they don't have the strength to cry any more.[5] Then comes the anger and recriminations. Someone is responsible. They have been faithful to David for eight years, following his lead at every turn. It is his idea to come to Philistia and now they have lost their wives and children. David may have lost as well, but their loss is greater.[6]

For the first time David faces the prospect of all-out revolt – some even talk of killing him. David becomes the focus of their fury.[7]

When pressure is at its greatest, the true foundations of our lives are uncovered. We read a simple yet profound statement about David at this moment of supreme crisis: 'David found strength in the Lord his God.'[8] We are not told the how and the why of this act – simply that David reaches out to God and finds what is needed.[9]

He calls for Abiathar the priest and uses the ephod and the stones Urim and Thummim, to discover God's will.[10] He asks God, 'Should we pursue the raiders – and if we do will we succeed?' The reply is favourable, and so he orders his men to go after the raiders.[11] These are Amalekites who lived south of Philistia. David has made cross-border raids and murderous attacks against them, so there is an element of revenge about the plundering of Ziklag.[12]

So hot is the chase that some of David's men collapse with exhaustion at a place called Besor Ravine. Overheated, dehydrated and emotionally stressed out, two hundred opt to remain while David and the bulk of his troops continue in their hunt for the Amalekite raiding party.[13]

We pause the story at this point and reflect on what has happened to David over the sixteen months he has lived in Philistine territory.[14]

- It has been a time of deception and killing
- David's compromise has taken him to the point of almost fighting against his own countrymen
- He and his men see their wives and children taken as hostages, their homes destroyed and property plundered
- His relationship with his loyal followers reaches an all-time low as David loses their trust and respect – and very nearly his life as well

Where did David get off God's pathway? When he took his eyes off the Lord and began constructing his own game plan.[15]

Meanwhile, Saul has continued his own journey away from God. The writer of the David story includes a curious incident that took place when David is with Achish.[16]

Samuel is dead and Saul feels spiritually exposed. With the Philistines preparing to attack Israel, Saul is desperate for some spiritual guidance. He looks for wisdom through prophets, the stones, Urim and Thummim and prayer, beseeching God for some revelation. But none comes.[17]

All the mediums and spiritists have been expelled from Israel, by the king's decree, though it is undoubtedly the result of Samuel's spiritual guidance.[18] Saul, in desperation, orders someone to be found who can contact Samuel beyond the grave. Saul is told a woman living in Endor practises secretly as a medium. He disguises himself and visits her. Asked if she will contact a dead person, she explains she is afraid – the king has decreed anyone doing so must die. Saul promises that no harm will come to her.[19]

When Samuel appears,[20] he has no comfort for Saul, who is begging for his guidance.[21] In line with the old prophetic denouncement,[22] God has rejected Saul and will take the kingdom from him and give it to David instead. Everything that Saul has fought against is now about to happen. Samuel states: 'The Lord will hand over both Israel and you to the Philistines,

and tomorrow you and your sons will be with me. The Lord
will also hand over the army of Israel to the Philistines.'[23]

Saul's response to this devastating news is to fall to the floor
in fear: 'His strength was gone, for he has eaten nothing all
that day and night.'[24] Eventually, he manages what is probably
his last meal on earth.[25]

Learning from the story

Once again the story of David offers contrasting lessons. In
this episode it is bound up with strength.

- Saul and losing strength
- David and finding strength

Saul and losing strength

Saul has been on a downward slide for a long time. His grasp
on the kingdom has been weakening. In one way, his desire to
discover a word from the Lord, as the Philistines marched out
against him, suggest that all is not lost. But here is no heartfelt
repentance or seeking after God's heart. Saul has shown before
that he sees the worship of Yahweh as a convenience rather
than a heart commitment. If this religion serves him then he
will embrace it – but on his own terms.[26]

At this stage of Saul's life, the curtain is about to come
down on the whole sorry story. He faces the biggest challenge
he has known. The Philistines are camped on his doorstep, his
courage has fled and he can't get God to work properly.[27]

So where does he turn in his need? To spiritism, even
though it is expressly forbidden by God and Saul himself, at
an earlier stage of his reign, had endorsed this biblical rule.

Everything that Saul has done on his slide away from God
has been driven by himself;

- His insane jealousy of David
- His attempts to take David's life

- His struggles to hold the throne and consolidate his power
- His attempt to break the silence of heaven and discover the future

Twenty-four hours before his life was ended in battle, the Bible spells out Saul's condition in four stark words, 'His strength was gone.'[28] Saul had relied on his own resources and used them all up. He was running on empty.

David and finding strength

The sixteen months in Ziklag were not the happiest of David's life. After years of walking with God and faithfully obeying him, David tried to run his own affairs. But when he found the thing in which he had placed his confidence – Ziklag – ruined and abandoned, David turned to God with a penitent heart. In total contrast to the strengthless Saul: 'David found strength in the Lord his God.'[29]

At the point of greatest need, David reached out to God and found grace, the currency of heaven, the basis on which God deals with us. Whatever we face today, if we come to Jesus empty-handed and in faith, then the Bank of Heaven will pay out.

Paul had his share of struggles, writing about a need that had bothered him for years. He had prayed but nothing happened. So strong was the problem, Paul labelled it, 'a thorn in my flesh, a messenger of Satan to torment me …'[30] Whatever this thing was,[31] it had become a real issue for Paul and he sought God earnestly for it to be lifted out of his life. The answer came to Paul: 'My grace is sufficient for you, for my power is made perfect in weakness.'[32] Paul discovered what David knew: 'When I am weak, then I am strong.'[33]

The question we face is this; in our weakness, whose strength are we relying on?

---

[1] 1 Samuel 29:2-5. David had succeeded in tricking Achish into thinking David's raids had been against his own people of Israel. In Achish's eyes, David had made himself so contemptible to his

fellow countrymen, he had no place to belong except among the Philistines (1 Sam. 27:10-12). His commanders were not as trusting.

2   1 Samuel 29:8. David's assertion of loyalty masks what must have been a difficult problem for him and his men. How could David be king of a country that he had betrayed?

3   1 Samuel 30:1.

4   1 Samuel 30:1-2.

5   1 Samuel 30:4. 'So David and his men wept aloud until they had no strength left to weep.'

6   The writer points out that David's two wives (and presumably their children) had also been taken as hostages (1 Sam. 30:5). But the anger of the men is so great, David's need is eclipsed.

7   1 Samuel 30:6.

8   1 Samuel 30:6.

9   The writer is ambiguous about what David did to find strength in God. But the psalms reveal enough of David's inner life for us to understand the importance that prayer, worship and meditation played for him in his spiritual journey.

10 For a reminder of how this worked see pages 64-65 and relevant footnotes.

11 This incident was a test of David's leadership skills. Some may note that when faced with a crisis, David responded with decisive action. But we should not miss the main point; David's primary action was to seek God.

12 1 Samuel 27:8ff. David had made raids against Amalekite towns and villages at the start of their stay at Ziklag.

13 1 Samuel 30:9-10. There may also be a strategic decision here about a wise deployment of force. To have two hundred men in reserve who have rested would have been a wise move if the Amalekites put up strong resistance.

14 1 Samuel 27:7 is specific about this time frame.

15 1 Samuel 27:1. A New Testament echo can be found in the story of Simon Peter walking on the water (Mt. 14:25-33). Peter walked well until he took his eyes off Jesus and became more aware of the elements. Similarly, David had lost sight of God and his decision to negotiate a deal with Achish was based on his own judgement as opposed to an express direction from the Lord.

[16] This incident is recorded in 1 Samuel 28:1-25. The opening verses set it in the context of David and his men winning Achish's trust to the extent that he offers David a job for life – as one of his personal bodyguards!

[17] 1 Samuel 28:5-6.

[18] The Law of Moses made it clear that such activities were against God's plan for the nation of Israel (see Ex. 22:18, Deut. 18:10-11).

[19] 1 Samuel 28:8-10. Saul once again shows how, for him, faith was something to be used as a commodity. He shows no compunction about using God's name in vain, let alone breaking his own decree about using mediums.

[20] This incident has prompted much discussion about the nature of life after death. One thing is apparent – the usual process undertaken by the woman was interrupted, causing her outcry and recognition of Saul. Some suggest that God miraculously allowed Samuel to speak from beyond the grave and this is what caused the woman such a shock. Her normal *modus operandi* involved deceiving spirits – this encounter was completely different.

[21] 1 Samuel 28:16-20.

[22] 1 Samuel 15:10-29. This word from God was given the last time Samuel saw Saul.

[23] 1 Samuel 28:19.

[24] 1 Samuel 28:20.

[25] 1 Samuel 28:21-25.

[26] It is worth retracing Saul's earlier steps that led to his rejection as king of Israel. First, his usurping of Samuel's authority (1 Sam. 13:7ff) and then his disobedience to the Lord's command (1 Sam. 15:1ff).

[27] Strange as this phrase may sound, it sums up Saul's attitude to God. When God is needed, he is expected to show up. There is no link in Saul's mind between his behaviour and seeking God's will. He does not exhibit faith as much as sheer presumption.

[28] 1 Samuel 28:20.

[29] 1 Samuel 30:6.

[30] 2 Corinthians 12:7.

[31] It seems possible that it was a physical problem, possibly affecting Paul's eyes, which caused great discomfort and inconvenience in his work for God.

[32] 2 Corinthians 12:9.

[33] 1 Corinthians 12:10.

13

Victorious

Listening to the story – 1 Samuel 30:11 – 31:13

Three small words sum up this episode in David's life – an episode that marked a defining moment changing his course irrevocably. Those three words are; 'David recovered everything.'[1] The episode covers two incidents, one where David is directly involved and the other where he is absent.

David and his men have returned to their temporary residence in the city of Ziklag only to discover the Amalekites have come against the city.[2] They have taken every living thing – women, children and livestock – and then set fire to the city leaving it a smouldering and deserted ruin. David rallies his men and sets out in pursuit of the Amalekite raiders. He and his men reach the Besor Ravine[3] where two hundred of them, weak from exhaustion, opt to stay and form a base camp. David and the bulk of his force, some four hundred men, pursue the Amalekite raiders.

Through a God-incidence,[4] they come across a man, an Egyptian slave, who has been taken ill and left behind by his Amalekite owner.[5] He makes a good recovery when he is fed and watered by David's men.[6] Glad to give his helpers any information they require, he informs them that this raiding party has made violent excursions to other places as well as Ziklag.[7]

David strikes a deal with him. The man will lead him to where the Amalekites are hiding on the condition that he will not be harmed and that David will not hand him back to his owner. The slave leads David and his men to the secret location where the raiding party are enjoying their spoils. They mount a ferocious attack that seems to have ended only when the youngest and fittest of the Amalekites flee in hasty retreat.[8]

By a miracle of God's grace, David recovers everything that had been taken by the Amalekite raiders.[9] David and his grateful men organise themselves for the return march to ruined Ziklag. As they reach the Besor Ravine, twisted human nature rears its ugly head. At the Ravine, the two hundred men, who had been exhausted and so stayed behind, are waiting. They are thrilled at the success of their comrades and welcome their wives and families with great joy.

But there are some among David's men who feel a sense of resentment towards those who opted out of the hard part of the mission.[10] They take the view that all that those who stayed behind deserve is the return of their wives and children. They are not entitled to a share in the copious amounts of plunder that have been taken from the defeated Amalekites.

David makes two interesting and important decisions – both of which have long-term results. They also reveal something of the character formation that God has been fashioning in his life.

His first decision is to reject the advice of the troublemakers. Everyone is to have equal shares in the divided spoil – including those who stayed back as well as those who fought. It is interesting to note that David bases his decision on two important factors. Firstly, the success they experienced was from the Lord alone.[11] Secondly, those who stayed behind were fulfilling an important task.[12] This was a landmark decision and became a feature of David's reign. What began as a gesture became enshrined as a law and one that stood for many years in Israel.[13]

David makes a second decision that day. When he returns to Ziklag, he decides to share out some of the blessings he has received. So he sends some livestock and goods to the leaders of his family tribe of Judah. With the gifts he sends a message: 'Here is a present for you from the plunder of the Lord's enemies.'[14]

These are friends who offered support and shelter to David and his men during these years when they have lived as fugitives. David sends his gifts to a wide variety of people across Judah as a mark of his gratitude and an acknowledgement of God's goodness to him.[15]

The second episode takes up the final chapter of the first book of Samuel and details the death of Saul, David's greatest enemy and Jonathan, his dearest friend.

David is absent when the terrible event happens on Mount Gilboa. Just as God has decreed, the Israelites suffer a crushing defeat against the Philistine army.[16]

The circumstances are described bleakly. Saul's three sons are killed in the battle and he is critically wounded by an arrow. Rather than be captured and tortured, Saul orders his armour-bearer to kill him. The terrified man refuses and so we are told that, 'Saul took his own sword and fell on it.'[17] His armour-bearer follows suit and the Bible records, 'So Saul and his three sons and his armour-bearer and all his men died together that same day.'[18]

This is a dark day for the nation of Israel and many of them abandon their homes and flee for their lives. The Philistine victory is total.[19]

When they come to strip the dead, the bodies of Saul and his sons are found. The news of their deaths is sent across Philistia and there is great rejoicing. Saul's armour is placed in an idol temple as a victory symbol and his headless body (and those of his sons) is hung up in a public square in a strategic town called Beth Shan.[20]

This sad chapter offers one glimmer of light as the brave exploits of the men of Jabesh Gilead are recorded. They repay a previous kindness from Saul's hands by rescuing the mutilated bodies and disposing of them in a more honourable fashion.[21]

So Saul's reign comes to an end. The man who started with such promise ends in such shame. The single biggest factor in

Saul's downfall can be summed up in one word. Disobedience. He missed God's best because he thought his own best was better.

As I mentioned at the start of this chapter, three small words sum up this episode in David's life: 'David recovered everything.'[22]

This episode changes the course of his life. He wins a great victory over the Amalekite raiders and regains his wives and children – but more than that, Saul is no longer king. The way to the throne of Israel stands open to David. What had been prophesied many years before is now able to be fulfilled.

He has refused to control events and seize power for himself. He has waited for God's timing. He has not tried to kill Saul – quite the opposite, he has saved his life on two occasions. David chooses to wait for God – and he recovers everything.

Saul ruins his life through disobeying God.

David finds his life through obeying God.

Learning from the story

At this decisive turning point in David's life three outstanding truths can be gleaned:

● Waiting for God
● Handling success
● Honouring others

Waiting for God

It had been a long time since Samuel's visit to Jesse's home in Bethlehem.[23] Over the intervening years, David must sometimes have wondered if the elderly Samuel had got it right when he had anointed him as the replacement king of Israel. Twice David had the opportunity to kill Saul and seize the throne by force – both times, he had refused.[24]

David is a wonderful example of an important spiritual quality – patience. It is a Spirit-produced fruit of character and, in common with its name, it takes time to grow.[25] We live in a world that deals with instant answers. Whatever the need, there's a speedy solution. But as many of us know from personal experience, some things are not dealt with instantly and therein lies our frustration. In a world with fast solutions the intractability of our problems can seem greater.

But the David story reminds us that the pathway of faith is steep, stony, narrow and long. It's the end destination that makes the journey worthwhile.

I often think about Easter Saturday – which seems to be the neglected day of the whole Easter celebration. We think of the Thursday and Jesus' last meal with his friends followed by the agonising prayer in the lonely garden called Gethsemane. We remember the Friday and the mockery, the scourging, the nails and the cross. We recall the darkened earth and the desolate cry, a torn curtain and bewildered disciples. Friday is so special we have hallowed it by calling it, forever, 'Good'. And then, of course, there is Sunday. The day of life, light and surprise. An empty grave and a risen Jesus.

But what about Saturday?

We read the Easter story backwards and it's rather like watching a film you've seen before. You arrive at a scary part – but you know everything turns out fine. Without trivialising the greatest event in history, that is how we so often view Good Friday – through the glorious lens of Easter Sunday. The horror of Good Friday is partly masked by the triumph of Easter Sunday.

But that first Easter Saturday was different. There was no hope of sunshine – it was lightless.

In spite of all that Jesus had said, the disciples hadn't listened. For them it was all over. What they had believed in and hoped for lay in ruins. Nothing made sense any more.

Evil had won.

God was dead.

I often think of Easter Saturday. It is a very important day because it helps make sense of some of the things I can't understand.

Auschwitz, Hiroshima, September 11, Dunblane. War, famine, earthquake, flood. The personal pain that so many of us carry – loss, grief and disappointment.

Easter Saturday sheds a ray of light on these dark places because it reminds us that waiting for God is worth it.

David learned that, too.

Handling success

Most of us would understand that adversity is one of the ways in which the Lord teaches and trains those who want to grow in godliness. David certainly met his fair share of adversity.

But have we understood that success can equally be used by God as a testing ground for character? How we handle success reveals what we are like inside. We even have a saying, 'She hasn't let success go to her head', which reveals we know what an intoxicating substance it can be. Rudyard Kipling refers to this truth in his famous poem, 'If',

> If you can dream – and not make dreams your master;
> If you can think – and not make thoughts your aim;
> If you can meet with Triumph and Disaster
> And treat those two impostors just the same...[26]

David, having defeated the Amalekites, took none of the glory of this triumph to himself. Instead, he pointed his men to the source of their success.[27]

David *had* recovered everything, but he didn't lose sight of the One who had made this happen. As the story unfolds we shall see how deeply ingrained this lesson had become in David's character.

It is important to consider how we handle success. Is there a sense of pride – or humble gratitude to God? Are we hardened in our triumph – or softened towards those who struggle as we once did? We prayed and trusted hard on the other side of this problem – how is our praying and trusting now? When we tell the story, how much glory goes to God?

Honouring others

There is a compelling human touch to this episode. It is the way in which David honours his friends. First, there is the far-reaching decision that those who stayed behind should have equal shares. Then there are the gifts David sends to his friends who have helped him through these difficult years.

It is good to honour those who have helped us because it shows an awareness of others and a sense of humility about our achievements. We are all indebted in one way or another to other people. There is no such thing as a self-made man or woman. Others have invested in our lives and David reminds us that it is important that such people are not ignored but properly recognised.

There are those who do the less glamorous jobs, such as staying back with the stuff. Theirs is not the glory of the battlefield, but the mundane routine of mucking out the donkeys. But as David decreed in the statute books, their role is just as important.

Then there are those who offer support, hospitality, friendship and shelter. We would be poorer without them and we should honour their contribution to our lives.

David remembered his friends and paid them due honour. In so doing, he proved the wise preacher of Ecclesiastes right when he said, 'Cast your bread upon the waters, for after many days you will find it again.' [28] David would soon discover that acts of kindness reap long-term rewards.[29]

We have noted the three words from the story that sum up this episode: 'David recovered everything.' But if we see this only in terms of his family and possessions we miss the point. God has been working on his character and waiting for the right time to hand him the throne. It has been a time of learning and growing, filled with days of pain and despair. David has made mistakes and lived with the results of them. In these experiences we find many parallels. God is able to work all things for our good.[30]

We draw hope from David's story.

[1] 1 Samuel 30:18.

[2] 1 Samuel 30:1ff.

[3] The brook Besor is the major wadi that drains the Negev and empties into the Mediterranean south of Gaza. It is a dry river bed for much of the year.

[4] A God-incidence is different from a co-incidence. The latter is a chance occurrence but a God-incidence is a set of circumstances that bear the divine fingerprint.

[5] 1 Samuel 30:11-15. One can only wonder at the heartlessness that lay behind this act.

[6] It is fascinating to note the precision of the narrator of 1 Samuel. It is not enough to say they fed him, he is keen that we know the exact contents of the meal (see 1 Sam. 30:12).

[7] 1 Samuel 30:14. The man identifies three other areas attacked by this group belonging to the Kerethites, the Calebites and the people of Judah (David's own tribe). They must have amassed a vast amount of plunder, including people and livestock.

[8] 1 Samuel 30:17. We are told the battle lasted 'from dusk until the evening of the next day'..Four hundred Amalekites fled on camelback – they are simply described as 'young men'.

[9] 1 Samuel 30:18-20.

[10] 1 Samuel 30:21-22. These malcontents are described (unflatteringly) as 'evil men and troublemakers'. Every group has them – including churches. And we must do all we can not to become influenced by them or to become one of them.

[11] 1 Samuel 30:23. David's response is forceful, 'No, my brothers, you must not do that with what the Lord has given us. He has protected us and handed over to us the forces that came against us.' It is not their might that has brought victory but the gracious intervention of the Lord on their behalf

[12] 1 Samuel 30:24. David articulates a vision for equality; 'The share of the man who stayed with the supplies is to be the same as that of him who went down to the battle.' If the troublemakers were alleging those who stayed back were cowardly, David destroys their argument. Those who remained behind were doing a job that contributed to the overall success of the team.

[13] 1 Samuel 30:25. The narrator acknowledged that it was a law still in force at the time he was writing. Equality of shares obviously

became an important feature of David's leadership and was passed on in succeeding generations.

[14] 1 Samuel 30:26. The elders of Judah are described as 'friends' of David. Even during these refugee years he had maintained his links and nurtured friendships. These were to prove vitally important in the future (see 2 Sam. 2:4ff).

[15] 1 Samuel 30:27-30. No less than thirteen towns or areas are listed as well as 'the other places where David and his men had roamed'. David had not forgotten his friends.

[16] 1 Samuel 28:1.9

[17] 1 Samuel 31:4 Saul commits suicide and so the phrase 'falling on one's own sword' passes into the English language.

[18] 1 Samuel 31:6.

[19] 1 Samuel 31:7.

[20] 1 Samuel 31:9-10. Beth Shan was located at the junction of the Jezreel and Jordan Valleys. This was a town at the crossroads and news of the public display of the corpses would have spread quickly with so many travellers passing through.

[21] Saul had rescued the people of Jabesh Gilead years before and they remained in his debt (see 1 Sam. 11:1-11). They acted with great courage in rescuing the bodies and honoured Saul as a king and his sons as princes – even to the extent of observing proper public mourning by fasting for seven days (see 1 Sam. 31:13).

[22] 1 Samuel 30:18.

[23] 1 Samuel 16:1-13.

[24] 1 Samuel 24:1-22, 26:1-25.

[25] Galatians 5:22.

[26] Rudyard Kipling (1865-1936) quoted in *Masterpieces of Religious Verse*, ed. James Dalton Morrison (Grand Rapids; Baker Book House, 1977), p279.

[27] 1 Samuel 30:23.

[28] Ecclesiastes 11:1. One possibility is that David's son, Solomon, was the author of this fascinating book, which lends a richer understanding of the analogy.

[29] Such wisdom is seen in the well known contemporary saying, 'Be nice to people when you're on the way up because you're sure to meet them again on your way down.'

[30] Romans 8:28.

14

Crowned

Listening to the story – 2 Samuel 1:1 – 3:39

The news of Saul's death reaches David in Ziklag from an unusual source. A young Amalekite brings news from the battlefield and presents David with Saul's crown and decorative armband. Unfortunately, he chooses to embellish the story of Saul's death by claiming that he delivered the blow that killed the king.[1]

David's reaction is the complete opposite of what the messenger and most observers would have expected. He and his men are filled with deep grief and immediately proclaim a period of official mourning.[2] The opportunist Amalekite is put to death for daring to do what David refused to do, raising his hand against the anointed of the Lord.[3]

David writes a beautiful lament for the lives of Saul and Jonathan. The words reveal something of David's generous heart as he mourns the loss of a man who was his sworn enemy and had made his life a misery for almost fifteen years.[4]

The next few chapters explain the civil war that raged in Israel, following the massive Philistine victory and Saul's death. David seeks God's guidance in these difficulties and is told to return to Israel and settle in Hebron within the tribal land of Judah. David and his family – together with his men and their families – leave Ziklag and return home.[5] Predictably, the men of Judah welcome David with open arms and lose no time in anointing him as king.[6] One of David's first acts is to honour the men of Jabesh Gilead who had retrieved Saul's body and buried it. He sends a message of thanks and encouragement.[7]

But not everyone was so keen to recognise David as the new monarch. Power-hungry Abner, who was commander of Saul's army, had somehow escaped the slaughter at Gilboa. He immediately establishes Ish-Bosheth, Saul's surviving son, as king over the rest of Israel, in the town of Mahanaim.[8]

The narrator adds a footnote – Ish-Bosheth's reign lasts two brief years. But David reigns as king of Judah for seven and a half years. The legacy of Saul's disastrous reign is a divided nation.[9] The depth of that division is revealed in an incident that occurs when David's men confront some of Ish-Bosheth's men at a lake. Their respective commanders, Joab and Abner, agree to a contest with twelve fighting men from each side in hand to hand combat.[10] This fierce fight eventually involves armed men from both sides in a contest so bloody that it passes into local folklore.[11]

An incident in that battle will have dire consequences for Abner later. In the fierce fighting he and his men are losing heavily. As he tries to escape, he is chased by one of Joab's brothers, Asahel. Asahel is fast and will not let Abner out of his sights.[12] Several times Abner urges Asahel to give up and let him go – but he steadfastly refuses. Eventually Asahel catches up with Abner, ready to kill him. But Abner thrusts the butt of his spear backwards into Asahel and he dies. His death stuns the pursuing army and they come to a halt at his body.[13] Joab and Abishai are determined to avenge their brother's death and pursue Abner. He and his men regroup on a hill and Abner calls down to his pursuers with a plea for the killing to stop. Joab and Abishai are persuaded – probably because they realise they are outnumbered by the re-formed group around Abner – and they withdraw to take their vengeance another day.

The final result of the battle is overwhelming. Three hundred and sixty of Abner's men lie dead as opposed to nineteen of David's army. Over the next couple of years, the civil war continues but with one continuous trend. David's position becomes stronger as Ish-Bosheth's becomes weaker.[14]

Three cameos chart the progress of this divided nation.

The first offers an insight into David and his family. When he arrives in Hebron he brings his two wives, Ahinoam and Abigail.[15] During this time he has married four more women who have borne him children. These marriages appear to have been prompted, partly, by a desire to make alliances with local states. Only the sons born to these women are listed, in accordance with the culture.[16] This is a time of consolidation and growth for David – and for his family. The long battle with Saul is over and the resistance from Ish-Bosheth is ineffective. Perhaps David's greatest pressure at this time is the need for continued patience until the throne can pass to him as God has promised.

The second cameo reveals what is happening in the other camp – and exposes the vulnerability of Ish-Bosheth's position. Abner has slept with a woman named Rizpah, who was one of Saul's concubines.[17] This was part of his plan to strengthen his own position. When Ish-Bosheth takes Abner to task for this extraordinary act of rebellion, he is brushed aside. Abner is furious that he should be challenged and threatens to hand Ish-Bosheth over to David. The narrator reveals the true state of Israel: 'Ish-Bosheth did not dare to say another word to Abner, because he was afraid of him.'[18] Ish-Bosheth may have had the title of 'King' – but the power lay with Abner.

The third cameo is a tale of revenge.[19] Abner sends a message to David requesting a meeting, to discuss how Abner can bring the whole of Israel under David's kingship. David agrees to the meeting on one condition; Abner brings with him David's estranged wife, Michal. As a snub to David, Saul gave her in marriage to a man called Paltiel.[20] To confirm his claim David sends a formal message to Ish-Bosheth demanding the return of his wife. It is unlikely that Ish-Bosheth knows of Abner's secret discussions with David – but he is powerless anyway. He meekly responds and Michal is sent back to David.

David and Abner eventually meet. Abner has convinced the elders in Israel that David will make a better king than Ish-Bosheth. The negotiations conclude with a feast. Abner agrees the terms and leaves with David's blessing to draw all Israel together for a coronation.[21]

Abner's ambitions are cut short by the intervention of Joab, determined to avenge the killing of his brother, Asahel. Joab is furious that David has accorded Abner safe passage, and accuses the king of gross naiveté, telling him that Abner's true motive was to spy out David's strength.

Joab (without David's knowledge) sends messengers after Abner, asking him to return to Hebron urgently.[22] When Abner returns, he is met at the gate by Joab. Calling Abner to one side, Joab stabs him to death.[23]

David is horror-struck at Abner's death. He distances himself from this act of violence, not least because of the political fallout it might create. He firstly pronounces a solemn curse on Joab and his family.[24] Second, he proclaims official mourning which he himself joins in as the king.[25] Third, he organises Abner's funeral and personally walks behind the coffin as a mark of respect. Fourth, David publicly sings a lament praising Abner and acknowledging the injustice of his murder.[26] David's public estimation of Abner is, 'Do you not realise that a prince and a great man has fallen in Israel this day?'[27]

His decisive action prevents an escalation in the civil war between Judah and the rest of Israel. Joab could have plunged the nation into a bloody, prolonged conflict. In God's providence, David acts as an inspired leader and the way is now open for what has been long promised to happen.[28] The throne that God promised David over twenty years ago is now within his sights.

Learning from the story

Four characters within these opening three chapters of 2 Samuel offer four insights into spiritual growth.

- David – and patience
- Abner – and power
- Asahel – and pursuit
- Joab – and passion

David and patience

If you have waited a long time for something, you will know the enormous sense of relief and achievement when that moment of fulfilment arrives. How do we feel, though, when we almost make the goal – but not quite? That is precisely where David is. Saul is dead and the way to the throne is open. David could confidently claim that his anointing by Samuel was his God-ordained ticket to power. But only his fellow clansmen take the bold step of making him king. The other eleven clans of the nation of Israel remain loyal to Saul's house, under the uncertain hand of his sole remaining son, Ish-Bosheth.

This delay must have been an enormous disappointment to David, testing both character and faith. He lived when many rulers believed 'Might is Right'. Some would even see this delay as a test of his leadership abilities. David's refusal to seize the initiative could be construed as weakness and render him incapable of ever ruling over the reunited twelve clans of Israel. But David is committed to waiting for God's moment, according to a divine timetable rather than his own.[29] During this time, which lasts for seven and a half years, David gets on with life.[30] His steadfast patience remains a challenging example.

Abner and power

The picture the Bible paints of Abner is not an attractive one. Living for power, he switched sides in order to obtain it. His life ended in assassination. He reminds us that power is a deceptive, corrupting drug. One of the most insightful comments about Abner's life comes in his angry response to Ish-Bosheth's challenge. 'May God deal with Abner, be it ever so severely, if I do not do for David what the Lord promised him on oath and transfer the kingdom from the house of Saul and establish David's throne over Israel and Judah from Dan to Beersheba.'[31]

Abner knew that God had promised the throne to David – yet his own ruthless pursuit of power had made him foolishly believe that he could stand against God's will.

His negotiations with David are not because he realised his disobedience and decided to change. He recognises an alliance with David was the best path to secure his own future. He relishes the role of king-maker[32] but it is personal power rather than the desire to do God's will that drives him.

Abner had been discipled by Saul – and his life showed it.

Asahel and pursuit

There is something wild about this young man Asahel. The three brothers Joab, Abishai and Asahel are described as 'The three sons of Zeruiah ...'[33] This made them David's nephews as Zeruiah was David's sister.[34]

Asahel possessed speed, agility and determination, 'as fleet-footed as a wild gazelle'.[35] Many have seen Asahel as the kind of dogged disciple that Jesus envisaged when he spoke those famous words: 'No-one who puts his hand to the plough and looks back is fit for service in the kingdom of God.' [36] Some may point out that Asahel's dogged pursuit led to his death. But Jesus called for those who would pursue him with a single-mindedness that pushes self interest and self-preservation to one side. It involves a level of dedication that is reckless about self. 'If anyone would come after me, he must deny himself and take up his cross daily and follow me.' [37]

Asahel reminds us that discipleship is about the dogged commitment of pursuit.

Joab and passion

Joab reminds us that blood feuds are, sadly, not a modern phenomenon. In his eyes he was doing the right thing – blood must be avenged by blood and his determination to kill Abner led him to this act of murder. But his actions had implications for David and the future. David's quick intervention prevented the situation deteriorating so far that the remainder of the tribes would not associate with him. After all, Abner was their chief negotiator.

Joab's passion for revenge blinded him to some important things. First, murder and lying are contrary to God's law. Second, two wrongs don't make a right. Third, the long-term goal of David becoming king over all Israel was going to be adversely affected by his actions.

Abner reminds us how dangerous it is to pursue power. Joab reminds us that passion can have a good or a bad effect on our lives. Being passionate for good things is commendable – but being passionate for bad reasons is dangerous.[38]

Joab had been unable to draw a line under the past and move on. His brother Asahel had been killed in the context of battle – and many more had died that day on the other side. But Joab was unable to accept that and his passionate desire for revenge crippled his outlook.

Four men who offer important perspectives on patience, power, pursuit and passion. They illustrate the truth of some words from the book of Proverbs:

Let your eyes look straight ahead,
fix your gaze directly before you.
Make level paths for your feet and take only ways that are firm.
Do not swerve to the right or the left;
keep your foot from evil. [39]

---

[1] 2 Samuel 1:2-10. This man may have been a looter stripping the dead who came across the fallen Saul and saw an opportunity for personal gain. It was common knowledge that Saul hated David and sought to kill him. If he could take David the good news that his enemy was dead, he might be suitably rewarded. He makes up the story of delivering the *coup de grace* with this in mind.

² 2 Samuel 1:11-12. There was no celebration at the death of an enemy but rather respect and a proper display of grief. The writer seems keen to point out that it was not merely the death of Saul and his sons that grieved them. Their brother Israelites who fought in Saul's army had been killed and the very description of them as 'the army of the Lord' reveals something of the sense of national shame at this defeat.

³ 2 Samuel 1:14-16. In David's view he was administering justice. Twice David had the opportunity to kill Saul – but his respect for 'the Lord's anointed' was so great, he let his enemy go free (1 Sam. 24:3-7, 26:8-11). His actions here need to be viewed against this background.

⁴ 2 Samuel 1:17-27. Eugene Petersen sees this lament as a pivotal point in the David story and believes it provides a model for grief in a world that trivialises loss and death. He notes that 70 per cent of the psalms are laments – many from David. Petersen, *Leap Over A Wall*, p115.

⁵ 2 Samuel 2:1-3.

⁶ 2 Samuel 2:4. Saul's death left a power vacuum. The men of Judah decided to act swiftly and acknowledge that their loyalty lay with one of their own – David.

⁷ 2 Samuel 2:4-7 and 1 Samuel 31:11-13. This was a genuine gesture from David – but also a shrewd one. He needed all the support he could get and by informing them of the decision of Judah to anoint him as king he was openly inviting the support of the people of Jabesh Gilead.

⁸ 2 Samuel 2:8-9. Abner saw Ish-Bosheth as someone who would provide him with the power he craved.

⁹ 2 Samuel 2:10. The difference in time length of their respective reigns may be explained by the fact that it took Ish-Bosheth (with Abner's help) five years to recover territory from the Philistines and rebuild the nation into some semblance of order.

¹⁰ 2 Samuel 2:12-32.

¹¹ The place was subsequently named The Field of Daggers – *Helkath Hazzurim* – (2 Sam. 2:16).

¹² 2 Samuel 2:18-23.

¹³ 2 Samuel 2:23. The death of Asahel made a deep impact on the exhausted soldiers. There is the suggestion (v24) that only Joab

and Abishai carried on chasing Abner. This may explain their decision to quit when Abner's men regrouped and they were outnumbered (v25).

14 2 Samuel 3:1.

15 2 Samuel 2:2. These wives and their children had been with David in Ziklag.

16 2 Samuel 3:2-5.

17 2 Samuel 3:7. To have sex with a royal concubine was a treasonous act. Abner's defiant refusal to accept any rebuke from Ish-Bosheth shows his naked desire for power and his refusal to conform to any rule that clashed with his own desires.

18 2 Samuel 3:11.

19 2 Samuel 3:12-39.

20 1 Samuel 25:44 records this rebuff from Saul. Why did David want Michal back? Was it because he genuinely loved her; to undo the stigma of Saul's insult; or to consolidate his claim to the throne? Or was it a complex mixture of all three?

21 2 Samuel 3:21. Abner has laid the groundwork before he meets David at Hebron. He negotiates with the elders of Israel and with the leading people of the tribe of Benjamin, Saul's clan, who would be most affected by the transfer of power to David and could be the targets of revenge killings. Abner would want to secure a deal preserving their lives. From his discussions with the elders of Israel it seems that David's popularity has grown to the extent that they want him to be their king (v17).

22 2 Samuel 3:26. Abner would easily be fooled by such a request. David could have summoned Abner back for further consultations.

23 2 Samuel 3:27.

24 2 Samuel 3:28-29.

25 2 Samuel 3:31-35.

26 2 Samuel 3:33-34.

27 2 Samuel 3:3.8

28 David makes no attempt to arrest and punish Joab for Abner's murder. However angry he feels at what had happened, he does not bring Joab to justice.

29 This principle is exactly how Jesus lived. When challenged about his miracles, Jesus revealed the game-plan of his ministry – John 5:19.

[30] 2 Samuel 2:11.

[31] 2 Samuel 3:9-10. Abner's exact words bear careful reflection. We learn three things: (1) the Lord's promise to David was no longer a secret; (2) Abner knew what God's will was in this matter – and so did Ish-Bosheth; (3) neither of them intended to do God's will even though they knew what it was.

[32] 2 Samuel 3:2.1

[33] 2 Samuel 2:18.

[34] 1 Chronicles 2:16.

[35] 2 Samuel 2:18.

[36] Luke 9:62.

[37] Luke 9:23.

[38] For an outstanding example, consider Jesus and his outburst at the famous Temple in Jerusalem (Jn. 2:13-17). His actions are seen as an example of passion for God and his glory.

[39] Proverbs 4:25-27.

15

Challenged

Listening to the story – 2 Samuel 5:1-25

David's years of preparation and testing lead to the events recorded in this chapter. His patience and willingness to wait for God's timing have been noted throughout the story. That patience bears fruit as he is crowned king of a reunified nation. But as with every new opportunity, fresh challenges arise. How will he handle power? Petersen expresses it this way, 'Up to this point we've been reading the story of the rise of David; from this point on we'll be reading the story of the reign of David.'[1]

Ish-Bosheth, son of Saul, was cruelly murdered by two of his trusted soldiers. Thinking David would reward them and welcome their crossing over to his side, they are confronted by an enraged David ordering their immediate execution.[2]

The death of Ish-Bosheth opens the way for the eleven tribes to express their wishes about their future monarch. A delegation of all the tribes meets with David at his headquarters in Hebron. They make a solemn announcement: 'In the past, while Saul was King over us, you were the one who led Israel on their military campaigns. And the Lord said to you, "You shall shepherd my people Israel, and you shall become their ruler."'[3]

Here – finally – is the acknowledgement of David as the Lord's choice. This leads to his third anointing for the task of kingship and it brings God's man to the throne of all Israel, at the age of thirty-seven years.[4] The divided nation is brought together under one king. They had been a scattered and divided people, a nation that needed David's skilful shepherding.

David is crowned king at Hebron and he enters into a covenant with the people to serve them honourably. The narrator adds some important chronological information at this stage of the story. Beyond the mathematics lies a testimony to the grace and kindness of the Lord. David was thirty years old when he became king over Judah. He reigned over his own clan for seven years and the united clans for thirty-three years. Thus his total reign was forty years long.[5]

Three significant achievements are recorded here. First, David's reunifying of the nation by peaceful means. Second, his establishment of Jerusalem as his capital, and, third, his comprehensive defeat of Israel's principal enemy, the Philistines. All of these achievements are seen as a direct result of the Lord's help. 'And he became more and more powerful, because the Lord God Almighty was with him.'[6]

Jerusalem was an ancient city that the Israelites had unsuccessfully tried to capture.[7] Strategically located within Benjamite territory, it would give a greater sense of belonging to the northern-based Israeli tribes. David finds it well-fortified and the Jebusites taunt that even a regiment of blind and lame people could ward his army off.[8]

But David refuses to attack along conventional lines. He discovers a shaft that provides fresh water to the city under siege. Somehow this is penetrated – and the city falls.[9]

David immediately begins various building projects and creates a new name for Jerusalem – the City of David.[10] He builds a palace with imported cedar wood and begins to establish his household through marriages which lead to the birth of various children.[11]

But alongside this period of construction and consolidation, there comes a distinct threat. The Philistines are aware of what is happening and plan to challenge David early in his reign. While he ruled the single tribe of Judah, he posed no great threat. But once the nation of twelve tribes has consolidated under his leadership, the Philistines take serious notice.[12] They march out against David in full force.[13] He responds by withdrawing his troops from Jerusalem, moving south to Adullam.[14] And he asks God what he should do and is assured it is right to attack the Philistines: the Lord will grant him success.[15]

David achieves a stunning victory. We are given just two details of the battle. First, we learn it was a heavy defeat for the Philistines because 'The Philistines abandoned their idols there, and David and his men carried them off.'[16]

A national 'god' was an important rallying point for people, having social as well as religious significance. To abandon your idols was like losing your flag. On this occasion, the surviving Philistine soldiers barely escaped. The second detail comes in the decision to name the location of the battle, Baal Perazim, which means, 'the Lord who breaks out'.[17] David commemorates this victory by acknowledging its true architect. As waters burst the river banks in flood season, so the Lord had 'broken out' in power against Israel's enemies. God endorsed his choice of new king by granting victory against the mighty Philistine army.[18]

Sometime later, the Philistine army regroup and decide once again to attack David and his troops.[19] Once more, the Valley of Rephaim is the scene for the battle.

David enquires of the Lord a second time.[20] The guidance he receives leads to a change of tactics. David is told to deploy some of his troops behind Philistine lines. They are to hide among a copse of balsam trees[21] until they hear the wind blow through the leaves, giving the sound of an army on the move. At this signal they are to attack quickly, as this will be a sign that 'the Lord has gone out in front of you to strike the Philistine army'.[22]

David does so and comprehensively defeats the Philistine army. David's grip as king is even more firmly established.[23] Reaching the throne, however, is not without its challenges. David, as a fugitive, was tested. Now on the throne, the tests continue. But, David succeeds in the challenges; the Lord is with him and grants him success.[24] He consolidates the nation, constructs a new capital city and conquers Israel's long-standing enemies.

Consolidation, construction and conquest. Three remarkable achievements in any ruler's book – and David accomplished all three under Yahweh's mighty hand.[25]

Learning from the story

This transition point in David's story offers some valuable lessons concerning spiritual growth. In particular three things stand out;

- David's story provides a picture
- David's story offers a pattern
- David's story illustrates a principle

David's story provides a picture

The three aspects of these early months of his reign are consolidation, construction and conquest. David had clear priorities as he came to the throne. These were God-shaped, not just bright ideas or the product of selfish desires. It wasn't just his agenda. Many people coming to power in similar circumstances would do several things. They would eliminate potential rivals, bolster their position by what is sometimes called 'cronyism' – paying back favours to those who helped them secure power, settle old scores, and begin to amass personal wealth and the trappings of prestige. The interests of the nation would come a long way down the list of most absolute rulers – as true now as then.

But David was made of different stuff. His kingship was God's gift, modelled on his experience as a shepherd. His pattern was that of a sheep-keeper rather than a despot.[26] This is an instructive model for any who are called to lead.

David's early months suggest a lesson in priorities. Needing to consolidate a divided nation, he decides to settle in

Jerusalem, to provide practically some sense of unity. But as with all relationships, he realised that this would be costly. Having chosen Jerusalem, he begins digging in for the long-term. Then came the phase of conquest with important battles fought and won. David gave himself to some important priorities with dedication and zeal.

As Petersen points out, David 'lengthened his stride and enlarged his embrace.'[27] He details what this personal growth involved for David – and for all who would follow David's God:

> When we grow, in contrast to merely change, we venture into new territory and include more people in our lives – serve more and love more. Our culture is filled with change; it's poor in growth. New things, models, developments, opportunities are announced, breathlessly, every hour. But instead of becoming ingredients in a long and wise growth, they simply replace. The previous is discarded and the immediate stuck in – until, bored by the novelty, we run after the next fad. Men and women drawn always to the new never grow up. God's way is growth, not change. Organic is a key image. Nothing from our past is thrown out with the garbage; it's all composted and assimilated into a growing life. And nothing – no 'moral', no 'principle' – is tacked on from the outside. David at thirty-seven was more than he was at seventeen – more praise, saner counsel, deeper love. More himself. More his God-given and God-glorifying humanity. A longer stride, a larger embrace.[28]

David's story provides a picture for a growing life.

David's story offers a pattern

Once a dream comes true, we can abandon values and friendships that kept us on track for our goal. Success can go to our heads. David had waited twenty long, frustrating years for his coronation. Anointed three times for this role over two decades,[29] now he had reached the summit. How would he handle it?

There is both a positive and a negative response, an encouragement to us in our own experience. Part of the frustration of the Christian life is our constant awareness of human frailty. Every time we achieve we are reminded of our failures. But this need not be a demoralising force, rather it can be a spur to keep us going in the right direction. The David story touches us because it is not an air-brushed portrait of unbridled success. The blemishes remain as a reminder that God is committed to less than perfect human beings with hearts turned towards him.

On the positive side, David has not become proudly self-sufficient. When confronted with the Philistine threat, David reverts to the patterns he has learned. Twice he seeks the will of God and obeys it.[30] This desire to live a God-directed life is at the core of David's being. There is the world of difference between aspiration and attainment. We can set ourselves goals and targets yet lamentably fail to meet them. David – in this aspect of his life – brings aspiration and attainment together. This is an earnest seeking of his face before major decisions are taken.[31]

On the negative side, David was influenced by his culture. His decision to take more wives and concubines was acceptable behaviour for a king, even *expected* behaviour. A major blind spot for David, this would have later implications. Rivalry among his many children would prove to be damaging, his own unbridled sexual appetite would almost cost his throne, and his example to his son, Solomon, laid dangerous foundations for the future. Perhaps, in later years, David became aware of his need to overcome blind spots. He certainly reflects this in one of his famous psalms: 'Who can discern his errors? Forgive my hidden faults.'[32]

J.B. Phillips' translation of the New Testament offers a powerful interpretation on avoiding the pressure to conform to the standards of the surrounding culture. 'Don't let the world around you squeeze you into its own mould, but let God re-mould your minds from within, so that you may prove in practice that the plan of God for you is good, meets all his demands and moves towards the goal of true maturity.'[33]

130 *The Story of David*

David's story offers us a pattern for our own lives. We see our own inconsistencies reflected and we are reminded of the constant choices we need to make daily, to pursue God and refuse to get squeezed into anyone else's mould.

David's story illustrates a principle

The principle comes from the lips of an anonymous prophet, 'Those who honour me I will honour, but those who despise me will be disdained.'[34] The illustration of the principle is spelt out in two phrases: 'And he (David) became more and more powerful, because the Lord God Almighty was with him.'[35] 'And David knew that the Lord had established him as King over Israel and had exalted his kingdom for the sake of his people Israel.'[36]

David had met the challenges of adversity well and God used the experiences to shape him. He now begins to face the challenges of success and starts in positive fashion. He sought to honour God and God in turn has honoured him. And here lies a truth for all to share.

Notice two things that David was clear about. He knew *who* lay behind his success – it was the Lord's doing – and *why* God had done this – for the sake of the Israeli people who needed a king who would lead well. After the disastrous reign of Saul, they needed some good years in their history. David was called to do a task he knew well.

God was asking him to shepherd a lost nation.[37]

---

[1] Petersen, *Leap Over A Wall*, p137.

[2] 2 Samuel 4:1-12. Once again, David's passion for justice is seen. There is nothing opportunist about his actions. He is consistent and deals with these men on the same basis as the man who (falsely) claimed to have killed Saul (v. 9-11).

[3] 2 Samuel 5:2.

[4] David was anointed three times. First, by Samuel (1 Sam. 16:13). Second, as king over the single tribe of Judah, his own clan, (2 Sam. 2:4). Third, as king over the whole nation of Israel (2 Sam. 5:3).

⁵ 2 Samuel 5:4-5.

⁶ 2 Samuel 5:10. Petersen, *Leap Over A Wall*, p135 points out another translation of this phrase suggests David moved forward, 'with a longer stride and a larger embrace'. His growth was not simply in power, but in experience, in spirituality, in life and in God.

⁷ Judges 1:8, 21. Judah temporarily occupied the city but the Benjamites failed to dislodge the controlling Jebusites.

⁸ 2 Samuel 5:6. There is some uncertainty about the exact meaning of this phrase but it seems probable that an insult was intended from people who felt they were in an impregnable city.

⁹ 2 Samuel 5:8. David is credited as having come up with the plan. Jerusalem's main water supply came from a spring outside the city walls. Archaeologists have discovered a number of shafts and tunnels that were used at different times to ensure a fresh water supply was brought into the city.

¹⁰ We meet another name for Jerusalem – Zion – which was probably the name of the hill on which the fortress stood. That is why in Scripture Jerusalem (or the heavenly or spiritual Jerusalem) is sometimes referred to as Mount Zion. Cf Psalm 9:11, 87:2, 137:3; Isaiah 28:16, 51:11; Joel 3:21; Zechariah 9:9; Romans 9:33, 11:26; Hebrews 12:22; Revelation 14:1.

¹¹ 2 Samuel 5:13-16. This is an example of becoming conformed to the prevailing culture. What David did by taking concubines and wives was accepted practice. A king would often consolidate his position by securing treaties with neighbours and sealing the deal with an arranged marriage. 'In one way, it was a recognized symbol of David's political stature in the Ancient Near East; but later chapters will show how much trouble was caused by the rivalry between his many sons.' *New Bible Commentary – 21st Century Edition* (4th Edition, 1994) Carson *et al* eds. (Leicester; IVP, 1994) p324. But see Deuteronomy 17:17 for God's express instructions on the matter. David (and his son, Solomon) chose to ignore these and in sowing the wind, reaped the whirlwind (see Hos. 8:7).

¹² 1 Samuel 29:1ff.

¹³ 2 Samuel 5:17.

¹⁴ 2 Samuel 5:17. The 'stronghold' could refer to his fortifications in Jerusalem (2 Sam. 5:7) but it seems more likely that he returned to his old military headquarters (1 Sam. 22:1-2). Both of the Philistine

attacks were in the Valley of Rephaim (2 Sam. 5:18, 22) which lay south of Jerusalem. David's relocation makes tactical sense.

15 2 Samuel 5:19.

16 2 Samuel 5:21.

17 2 Samuel 5:20 and NIV margin.

18 1 Samuel 31:1ff It is impossible to overstate what this victory would have meant for David's personal standing as the newly crowned king. The defeat at Gilboa was a national disaster. Saul and three of his sons were killed and the army routed. This first major test of David's authority consolidated his throne.

19 2 Samuel 5:22. The writer does not say how long after the defeat at Baal Perazim this took place, but the inference of the text suggests there was not a huge time lapse. Perhaps the capture of their idols made the Philistines decide on a swift follow-up attack. They may have felt religiously powerless without their idols and seen the need to get them back quickly, no matter what the cost.

20 2 Samuel 5:23. David avoids the trap of 'familiarity breeds contempt'. He patiently seeks God afresh, recognising that yesterday's guidance will not do for today. He needs God's mind on this matter right before him.

21 These are baka-shrubs from which sap or resin comes.

22 2 Samuel 5:24.

23 2 Samuel 5:25.

24 2 Samuel 5:10.

25 'The fact that a foreign king, "Hiram king of Tyre sent messengers to David" (11), demonstrates the growing power and importance both of David himself and the nation he ruled. For most of the 10th century BC, Israel was the most powerful nation in the whole region. The biblical writer acknowledges David's skills and achievements but he credits them ultimately to "the LORD God Almighty" (10)'. *New Bible Commentary, 21st Century Edition* (4th Edition, 1994) Carson et al eds. (Leicester; IVP, 1994), p324

26 2 Samuel 5:2. This was the basis of David's call to lead. He was to be the Shepherd King.

27 See footnote 6.

28 Petersen, *Leap Over A Wall*, p136.

29 See footnote 4.

30 2 Samuel 5:19, 23.

[31] For an example of how David enquired of God in earlier years, see 1 Samuel 23:2, 4.

[32] Psalm 19:12.

[33] J.B. Phillips, *The New Testament in Modern English* (London: Geoffrey Bles, 1960). Quotation taken from Romans 12:2, p332.

[34] 1 Samuel 2:30. This anonymous 'man of God' came to the priest Eli and brought an uncomfortable message of impending judgement on a corrupt priesthood. Samuel, David's mentor, was to play a significant part in the unfolding of this prophecy.

[35] 2 Samuel 5:10.

[36] 2 Samuel 5:12.

[37] 2 Samuel 5:2.

16

Tested

Listening to the story – 2 Samuel 6:1-23

David makes Jerusalem his kingdom's capital, but wants it to be more than a political centre. The worship of Yahweh must be central to the life of the nation, with Jerusalem as its centre-point.

The Ark[1] was the focal point for worship of Yahweh, but it had been left in a town called Baalah.[2] Saul failed to recover it and it lay in Abinadab's house, guarded but neglected.

David saw the return of the Ark as a major opportunity to restore some spiritual life to Yahweh's people. It was a symbolic act with potentially large consequences; unity of the people, revival of religious worship and the drawing together of the twelve tribes.

David made special arrangements to transport the Ark on a brand-new cart the ten miles to Jerusalem, where a special tent was erected.[3]

This was no solemn religious event. David wanted the occasion to draw the nation together in a loud celebration – and he was not disappointed. 'David and the whole house of Israel were celebrating with all their might before the Lord.'[4]

Then an unforgettable incident occurs. Uzzah[5] – one of Abinadab's sons – is transporting the Ark. Things become boisterous, the oxen pulling the cart stumble and the Ark is at some risk. Uzzah reaches out to steady the Ark with his hand[6] and 'The Lord's anger burned against Uzzah because of his irreverent act; therefore God struck him down and he died there beside the ark of God.'[7]

David reacts with anger and fear: anger[8] at Uzzah's untimely death and what he sees as God's unfair treatment, and fear because he recognises God's power, bound up with the Ark. He wonders what he can do next. Having moved the Ark from where it had been undisturbed for twenty years, he is reluctant to take it further.[9]

Close by was the house of a man named Obed-Edom, a Levite, the tribe from which priests were drawn.[10] David leaves the Ark safely with him, while he decides what to do next.

In the intervening weeks several things occur. Obed-Edom and his family receive unprecedented blessing.[11] Then, David thinks seriously about what had happened. He takes some advice and looks at the Holy Books of Moses to learn about the Ark of the Covenant.[12] He decides to try again to move the Ark to Jerusalem, with proper preparation and under Levite supervision.[13]

As the joyful assembly makes its way up to Jerusalem[14] sacrifices are offered at various points. David, as the king, takes part, dressed in a linen ephod[15] rather than in his royal robes. He is an enthusiastic worshipper: 'David, wearing a linen ephod, danced before the Lord with all his might.'[16]

Not everyone is keen to see King David dressing and behaving in such an unkingly way. Michal[17] is watching the parade from the palace, 'And when she saw King David leaping and dancing before the Lord, she despised him in her heart.'[18]

The Ark is safely returned and placed inside the special tent. More offerings are made and David pronounces a final blessing on the people.[19] This was a day to be remembered!

Unfortunately, he doesn't find such an enthusiastic welcome at home. David returns to the palace to 'bless his household'.[20] But Michal accuses him of behaviour below his station as king, saying 'You have made yourself look common.'[21]

David responds to Michal's criticism by highlighting some important truths:[22]

- David is acting out of what his heart feels – he is offering his worship before the Lord, not as a crowd-pleaser.
- The Lord has appointed David as king over Israel. Michal's father, Saul, had been rejected and no-one from his family has been appointed in his place.
- If his lack of dignity bothers Michal, then she should know that David will do other things that might shock her.
- The slave girls that Michal claim will despise David for his actions will, in fact, honour him.

The narrator adds a comment that helps us understand the significance of this incident. 'Michal daughter of Saul had no children to the day of her death.'[23] It may have been recorded to show why no-one from Saul's line made a claim to the throne in later years. Michal was the best hope of this happening – and this incident closed the door on that possibility.[24]

David is a wiser man in the ways of God – but his wisdom has been hard won.

Learning from the story

This episode in David's life highlights two extremes that we face in our relationship with God – the extremes of familiarity and formalism.

Familiarity

The death of Uzzah throws up big questions! It is mysterious and awesome. Petersen offers a helpful comment, drawing on the reflections of other generations:

> Over the centuries, as the Christian imagination has reflected on Uzzah's death, one insight has appeared over and over: it's fatal to take charge of God. Uzzah is the person who has God in a box and

officiously assumes responsibility for keeping him safe from the mud and dust of the world.[25]

He sees in Uzzah's story, a warning we all should heed,

Holy Scripture posts Uzzah as a danger sign for us: 'Beware God'. It's especially important to have such signs posted in places designated for religious worship and learning …

We begin by finding in God a way to live rightly and well, and then along the way we take over God's work for him and take charge of making sure others live rightly and well. We get the idea that we're important, self-important, because we're around the Important.

Religion is a breeding ground for this kind of thing. Not infrequently these God-managing men and women work themselves into positions of leadership. Over the years the basics with which they began, the elements of reverence and awe, the spirit of love and faith, erode and shrivel. Finally there's nothing left. They're dead to God. [26]

David's motives were good – the recovery and restoration of the Ark was an important part of the divine agenda. But God's work must be done in God's way if it is to be done well. David did not 'enquire of the Lord' as he usually did. He failed to consult the Holy Books of Moses[27] which would have shown him what was required, and he was ignorant of the fact that recently a large group of Israelites had died after tampering with the Ark.[28]

The solemn lesson of this most difficult episode is wrapped up in the old saying 'familiarity breeds contempt'. David – and those around him – were becoming over-familiar with holy things. They believed the return of the Ark was simply an event that needed some slick stage-management. Holiness has an awesome power, as Isaiah and John discovered to their cost.[29]

Scripture repeats the phrase: 'The fear of the Lord is the beginning of wisdom.'[30] The Bible teaches the transcendence of God – he is high above our thoughts and ways.[31] Yet, in Jesus, we discover the immanence of God. He is Immanuel, the 'with us God'.[32] The Most High God, yet the most nigh God. The two truths must be held in equal tension.

Every generation makes its own mistakes. Our generation expresses the immanence of God at the expense of his transcendence, so reversing the previous generation's extreme where God was seen as totally other and unknowable.

Familiarity is a dangerous extreme.

Formalism

Here is the opposite end of the scale, seen in the reaction of Michal, David's wife.

The period of three months when the Ark was deposited at the home of Obed-Edom was an important growing time for David. It is thought that one of his psalms[33] was composed at this time, which reveals a humble attitude:

> Let us go to his dwelling-place;
> let us worship at his footstool –
> arise, O Lord, and come to your resting place,
> you and the Ark of your might.
> May your priests be clothed with righteousness;
> may your saints sing for joy.
> For the sake of David your servant,
> do not reject your anointed one.[34]

David admits the mistake he made first time around in transporting the Ark: 'It was because you, the Levites, did not bring it up the first time that the Lord our God broke out in anger against us. We did not enquire of him about how to do it in the prescribed way.'[35] The account in 1 Chronicles details the elaborate preparations that were made on this second attempt to return the Ark to Jerusalem.

Scripture shows David as a man of intense passion, so his decision to abandon kingly robes and dance 'with all his might' is not a complete shock.[36] Some have seen in his example a suggestion that all Christians should dance as part of their worship of God.[37] Certainly the picture of unrestrained, uninhibited praise to God is recorded for us as a good example.

But Michal acts like the older brother in Jesus' story of the forgiving father.[38] She is not happy at what she sees. Petersen quotes a famous preacher of a previous generation, Alexander Whyte: 'Those who are deaf always despise those who dance.'[39]

Her despising heart was caused by jealousy (envying David's relationship with God), pride (implicated and dragged down by David's behaviour), and resentment (left out of the parade).[40] From this complex cocktail came an angry reaction – that would have serious implications for Michal's life. She challenged the king and her actions became public knowledge.

For Michal there was an acceptable way of receiving back the Ark and David had chosen to ignore it. But this was more than a clash of opinions over good manners. There was an issue between them over dignity. She felt he had lowered himself as king, acting in an unseemly way. She was being judgmental – which distorts the true picture.

There was a similar clash between Judas Iscariot and Mary, the sister of Lazarus.[41] Mary broke an expensive bottle of perfume and anointed the feet of Jesus, wiping them with her hair. This extravagant act of worship was prompted by Jesus' action in raising her dead brother Lazarus to life again. But Judas – like all formalists – missed the point. His objection (on the surface) was pure economics. Such a gesture was an expensive waste. Fortunately Jesus looked beyond the gesture to the heart. He saw both Mary's worshipping heart and Judas' lying heart.

We are told that in the Church, 'everything should be done in a fitting and orderly way'.[42] That is God's mind on the matter. But lest we make an idol of form, we are warned that, 'the letter kills, but the Spirit gives life'.[43] The twin signs of formalism and familiarity mark out some dangerous territory to be avoided for those who would be true lovers of God. Don Carson offers this comment:

Here is a profound lesson. At one level, doubtless God approves childlike praise and enthusiastic zeal. But he expects those with authority among his people to know what his Word says and obey it. No amount of enthusiasm and zeal can ever hope to make up for this lack. Zeal that is heading in the wrong direction never reaches the goal. It must either be redirected in the direction staked out in God's Word, or, however enthusiastic, it is still wrong-headed and misdirected. There is no substitute for faith working itself out in informed obedience.[44]

---

[1] The Ark of the Covenant was a central feature of the worship life of the people of Israel (see Ex. 25:1ff). Petersen, *Leap Over A Wall*, p148 offers the following description; 'The Ark of the Covenant was a rectangular box, not quite four feet in length and a little over two feet in depth and width. It was constructed of wood and plated with gold. Its lid of solid gold was called the mercy seat. Two cherubim, angel-like figures at either end, framed the space around the central mercy seat from which God's word was honoured. The Ark contained three items: the tablets of stone that Moses had delivered to the people from Sinai; a jar of manna from the wilderness years of wandering; and Aaron's rod that budded.'

[2] 1 Samuel 4:1 – 7:2 gives details of the Ark's capture and subsequent events.

[3] 2 Samuel 6:17. Other plans emerged later for a more permanent location for the Ark.

[4] 2 Samuel 6:5.

[5] 1 Samuel 7:1 states Eleazar son of Abinadab was 'consecrated … to guard the Ark of the Lord …'

[6] The reference to Uzzah using his hand to steady the Ark is not found here but in the parallel passage at 1 Chronicles 13:10.

[7] 2 Samuel 6:7 does not give the details on how Uzzah died. Was he crushed by the cart or struck dead on the spot?

[8] We read two statements in two verses, 'Then David was angry … David was afraid of the Lord …' (2 Sam. 6:8,9).

[9] 2 Samuel 6:9 – David asks the question, 'How can the Ark of the Lord ever come to me?' What else might happen if someone acted wrongly?

10 We know Obed-Edom was a Levite from the details of the Levite families recorded in 1 Chronicles 26:4.

11 2 Samuel 6:11. The Ark remained with this family for twelve weeks and in that time the whole household was affected for good.

12 This enquiry on David's part is seen in the parallel passage of 1 Chronicles 15, in particular in verse 13 where David acknowledges his failure to enlist the Levites to help.

13 The parallel passage of 1 Chronicles 15 goes into greater detail at this point. The priest and Levites undergo spiritual preparation and carry the Ark on their shoulders in the way prescribed by the Lord through Moses. David's first attempt involved carrying the Ark on a cart, albeit a new one. But such an action betrayed a careless heart (see 2 Sam. 6:3). Music was a major part of the celebration. But although it was solemn, it was not a miserable occasion – there was great rejoicing (see 2 Sam. 6:12; 1 Chr. 15:25) because the return of the Ark symbolised the presence of Yahweh among his people.

14 2 Samuel 6:12: already Jerusalem is being called 'The City of David'.

15 A linen ephod was a close fitting, sleeveless garment worn by priests in their official duties (1 Sam. 2:18; Ex. 28:6-14).

16 2 Samuel 6:14.

17 Michal had been sent back to her first husband, David, after her father had married her off to another man as a snub to his son-in-law.

18 2 Samuel 6:16.

19 2 Samuel 6:19 – the narrator faithfully records that 'a loaf of bread, a cake of dates and a cake of raisins' was given out 'to each person in the whole crowd of Israelites, both men and women.'

20 2 Samuel 6:20. This may mean to offer a prayer of blessing in the name of Yahweh as he did for the people (v 18), to distribute some bread and cakes – or to pass on some of the joy of the day to his wives and children.

21 The issue is not that David took his clothes off and offended public decency. It was the laying aside of his royal robes and acting as one of the people that upset Michal.

22 2 Samuel 6:21-22.

[23] 2 Samuel 6:23. We are not told if this means she was struck barren as a punishment or if it marked a severe deterioration in her relationship with David so they no longer slept together.

[24] *The New Bible Commentary, 21st Century Edition* (4th Edition, 1994) Carson *et al* eds. (Leicester; IVP, 1994), p325, states, 'Many later chapters are concerned with David's sons and with their ambitions to become king. If Michal had ever had a son, he would have had a strong claim to the throne, as Saul's grandson and David's son. No such son was born.'

[25] Petersen, *Leap Over A Wall*, p150.

[26] Petersen, *Leap Over A Wall*, p151.

[27] The Law of Moses laid down precise instructions of how the Ark was to be carried and who was entitled to do it. Exodus 25:14-15; Numbers 3:30-31, 4:15, 7:9.

[28] 1 Samuel 6:19. When the Ark had first been returned by the Philistines, some Israelite men from Beth Shemesh took a curious look inside. Seventy of them were struck dead as a direct result. 'The people mourned because of the heavy blow the Lord had dealt them, and the men of Beth Shemesh asked, "Who can stand in the presence of the Lord, this holy God? To whom will the ark go up from here?"' (vv 19-20). The Ark had come to rest in Abinadab's house because the inhabitants of Beth Shemesh wanted it removed from their village (v 21).

[29] Isaiah's vision of God led to an immediate confession of his own sinfulness and need (Is. 6:5). The revelation of Jesus in his heavenly splendour caused John to fall down 'as though dead' (Rev. 1:17).

[30] Proverbs 9:10, 15:33, 1:7.

[31] Isaiah 55:8.

[32] Isaiah 7:14.

[33] It is thought that Psalm 132 (one of the pilgrim 'Songs of Ascents') was written at this time. See verse 6: Jaar is also known as Kiriath Jearim or Baalah.

[34] Psalm 132:7-10.

[35] 1 Chronicles 15:13.

[36] 2 Samuel 6:14.

[37] I am not convinced this is what the passage actually teaches us. Dancing was an essential part of Hebrew culture – for men and

women. David was worshipping within the framework of his culture. He was probably good at it! Enthusiasm minus skill makes a sorry sight. Enthusiasm plus skill is a different matter (1 Chr. 15:22).

38 Luke 15:28ff. Jesus used the figure of the older brother in the story to expose the dead formalism of the religious leaders of his day.

39 Petersen, *Leap Over A Wall*, p153.

40 2 Samuel 3:15ff.

41 John 12:1-8.

42 1 Corinthians 14:40.

43 2 Corinthians 3:6.

44 D.A. Carson, *For the Love of God*, Volume 1, (Leicester: IVP, 1998), daily reading comment for 20 November.

17

Refused

Listening to the story – 2 Samuel 7:1-29[1]

David's battle for survival is over. He is established on the throne in Jerusalem. God has enabled him to bring a period of peace and stability to the nation of Israel.[2] Turning his attention to the Ark that he has brought to Jerusalem,[3] David considers building a more permanent home for it, a temple for the worship of Yahweh.[4]

He tells Nathan who, as a prophet of the Lord, has a special advisory role in the royal court.[5] David's concern is that he's living in a finely constructed palace while the Ark is housed in a tent! He tells Nathan his desire to build a permanent Temple.

Nathan advises, 'Whatever you have in mind, go ahead and do it, for the Lord is with you.'[6] But that night, the Lord gives him a very different message.[7] In summary,[8] the Lord's message to Nathan says:

- David is not the one to build the Temple
- God has never asked any of his servants to build a permanent structure
- The Lord chose David and will make his name great in world history
- The Lord will settle the nation of Israel in peace

- The Lord will establish a house for David – his son, who will succeed David as king, will be the one to build a permanent Temple
- The Lord will guide and correct[9] David's son and establish his kingdom – for ever[10]

Next morning, Nathan gives David this message from the Lord.[11] David's response is that of someone overwhelmed by God's outrageous grace. He goes to the tent housing the Ark and sits down in the presence of the Lord.[12] He preserved for us the words of a prayer he offered.[13] David feels overwhelmed by the sheer goodness of the Lord, 'Who am I, O Sovereign Lord, and what is my family, that you have brought me this far?'[14]

The remainder of his passionate prayer expresses what David felt at receiving this message from God.

- As if the blessings to date are not enough, the Lord has spoken about blessings for the future
- This revelation is 'for the sake of your word and according to your will'[15] – David sees a bigger plan unfolding here other than his personal blessing
- There is no-one like the Lord
- There is no other nation like Israel – specially chosen and blessed of God
- He calls on the Lord to 'do as you promised', [16] and thus to magnify his name
- David concludes by humbly seeking the blessing of the Lord on his household – in order that God's purposes may be fulfilled

David enjoyed a rich intimacy with God and his psalms reveal something of the texture of his worship life. But David is being turned down by God. His plans – which looked commendable – did not fit God's overall plan. How will he cope with refusal? His prayer answers the question. David is overwhelmed with God's importance rather than his own.

The message from God is very clear. David will not build a Temple for the Lord – his son who will succeed him will achieve this. But the Lord will bless David's dynasty and make his name great. Through this, the whole nation will be blessed and David's throne will be established for ever. In political and spiritual terms, the Lord handed David a blank cheque.[17]

We view the prophecy with the benefit of three thousand years of hindsight. David's throne – in terms of human dynasty – has not endured forever. Nor is the Temple built by his son Solomon still standing. We see in the message Nathan received and conveyed a double interpretation. At one level, the prophecy was fulfilled through Solomon's accession to the throne and the construction of his magnificent Temple. But at a deeper level, this promise of an everlasting Kingdom was to be fulfilled through 'great David's greater son', the Lord Jesus Christ.[18]

David's dream of a Temple is eclipsed by a greater building project. God's ultimate intention is for a house made up of living stones drawn from every people group with his beloved Son, Jesus, at its very centre.[19]

Learning from the story

The episode recorded in this chapter illustrates the essential difference between a good idea and what we might call 'a God idea'. Within that illustration we discover parallels for all who desire to love God.

In particular, four things stand out from the narrative as critical in David's growth in the life of faith:

- A teachable spirit
- A humble heart
- A faithful prophet
- An eternal perspective

A teachable spirit

A teachable spirit is revealed through the ability to learn and grow. David shows this in a number of ways – his willingness to seek Nathan's counsel, his ability to accept the change of plan and his humility in receiving a refusal of his original intention. But perhaps the most significant example is shown by the change of language in the passage.

There are three phases in the story. Phase 1: David announces his intention to Nathan. David wants to do something for God: 'Implicit in the comparison between his palace of cedar and the tent of the Ark is the judgment that David is now housed better than God, that David has achieved a better standard of living than God, and that from David's position of strength he can now do something significant for God.'[20]

Phase 2: the stunning revelation unloaded on Nathan. Study of the text reveals a picture of the Lord in action – past, present and future are all covered in this sweeping declaration. God's actions in the history of Israel, his choice to take David from shepherding and place him on the throne and God's plans for the future are all revealed. It has been pointed out that in the message to Nathan, God is the first person subject of no less than twenty-three verbs.[21]

Phase 3's language is no less significant. David sits before God in the place of prayer. This is more than a religious posture – it shows where David has travelled from in his journey with God. 'Whereas before, David was full of himself, now David is full of God. Seventeen times David refers to God by name – God, Lord God, Yahweh, God of Hosts; he uses the personal pronoun for God an additional forty-five more times.'[22]

Our mouths reveal much about our inner life – as Jesus tells us.[23] The language of the three phases of this episode reveal David's teachable spirit and pose a challenging question. What matters most – my plans for God – or God's plans for me?

A humble heart

Kings in the ancient Near East were not renowned for flexibility. Most were despots, crushing any who opposed their plans. David had spent years running from Saul who was

determined to annihilate the one he saw as the principal threat
to his power base. Now David has been thwarted in his plans
– and they were not bad plans. His ambition to build a temple
for God was full of high ideals, but he was the wrong man for
the job.[24]

It is never easy to be turned down. It throws up old insecurities and unhealed wounds. But David's fugitive years have
forged a strong faith. Part of that process is seen in the fruit of
humility in his life. He has already told his wife Michal that he
doesn't fear of what people think[25] and this liberates him to
concentrate on pleasing God.

The humble heart of David is seen in his response to
Nathan's message. We see it in his actions and hear it in his
words. His actions take him to the tent where the Ark is being
kept and he takes the posture of prayer. There is no sulking
over the rejection of his plans. His opening words show the
humility he feels; 'Who am I and what is my family that you
have blessed us at all?'

You can almost touch David's feelings at being overwhelmed by grace. And the spirit of his prayer is summed up,
'And if this were not enough…' [26]

David knew where the real power lay and he kept this
important perspective at what could have been a dangerous
time of disappointment for him. How we handle disappointments reveals the true place God has in our hearts and how far
we have come in the school of humility.

A faithful prophet

Where would David have been if it were not for the faithful
Nathan? His presence tells us that the king was looking
beyond himself for the resources he needed to fulfil his duty.
It is one thing to express dependence on God – quite another
to live out the implications.

David's first step is to seek the prophet's advice.[27] Nathan
is from the school of faithful prophets rather than the
rubber-stamping kind. Having given what he believed to be
the obvious response, he is courageous enough to come back

to the king with a fresh word from God. No human being can ever claim infallibility or behave as if they possess a hotline to heaven. Nathan was humble and this made him a safe pair of hands, reminding us that vulnerability is never a sign of failure in a leader. To acknowledge weakness is an important part of strong leadership.[28]

We all need Nathans in our lives. They may have some official title such as pastor, vicar or priest – or they may simply be people God has chosen to bring alongside as friends. But our willingness to receive from such friends is evidence of the teachable spirit and humble heart. Perhaps they will bring confirmation and support. Perhaps they will bring challenge and rebuke, as faithful Nathan did.[29] Perhaps it is the word of redirection that David accepted here.[30]

The important thing is that – whatever message they bring – we all need faithful prophets.

An eternal perspective

How much did David grasp of all that the Lord said? He understood enough to acknowledge how extraordinary this revelation was. It is rare for God to reveal his future plans for an individual.[31] What is striking about this episode is David's willingness to abandon his plans for God's. All too often we bring our ideas and seek God's divine seal of approval. Our seeking of God's will ends up as nothing more than a selfish pursuit of endorsement for what we are determined to do anyway. As we have already acknowledged, disappointment is an accurate means of testing our flexibility and obedience.

David was a strong man with great influence. But he had not lost his understanding of who had brought him to this place. He had seen what power had done to Saul and remained determined to be a different kind of king. I describe this as possessing an eternal perspective as it seems to summarise what this involves; an acknowledgement that God is sovereign over all, and a willingness to live out the prayer that says, 'Your kingdom come, your will be done on earth as it is in heaven.'[32]

When we are able to pray that over our most precious of plans, we are truly living with an eternal perspective. For David this led to something bigger and better than he could have imagined. As so often happens, when we exchange our plans for God's, we discover the blessing flows beyond ourselves to touch many more lives. It is said that, 'The good is the enemy of the best.'

David relinquished a good idea for a God idea, and so managed to turn refusal into a party when it could easily have ended up a wake.

---

1   This chapter is key, not only in the unfolding story of David, but in terms of Old Testament revelation generally.

2   2 Samuel 7:1. The description of David 'settled in his palace and the Lord had given him rest from all his enemies around him' signals a period of peace and blessing for the whole nation.

3   2 Samuel 6:17.

4   The 'Tabernacle' or 'Tent of Meeting' was a portable structure used for worship (Ex. 33:7-11, 35:1ff). During the wilderness wanderings, it provided focus for worship. It continued to be used after Israel settled in Canaan. During the period of the Judges it was based at Shiloh (Josh. 18:1). In Saul's reign it was based at Nob (1 Sam. 21; Mk. 2:25-26) and later at Gibeon (1 Chr. 16:39).

5   2 Samuel 7:2. Nathan appears from nowhere in the David story. He has a crucial place in the royal court. David wanted to have a spokesman for the Lord in his inner circle. The fact that David consults Nathan on his building plans for the Temple reveals how seriously he took the prophet's advice.

6   2 Samuel 7:3. From Nathan's perspective, this was one of the easier issues on which to comment. His job must have meant considerable thought and prayer at different times. It was obvious to him that what David had in mind was 100 per cent in accordance with the Lord's will.

7   2 Samuel 7:4ff. 'The word of the Lord came ...' is a form of biblical shorthand to indicate God speaking – for example, I Kings 18:1; Micah 1:1.

8   2 Samuel 7:5-16.

⁹ 2 Samuel 7:14. This concept of correction and punishment by 'floggings inflicted by men' can create confusion. It doesn't refer to the Lord Jesus. He was ill-treated as part of his willing sacrifice of himself on our behalf. But he was not punished for things he had done wrong – he was acting as sin-bearer for all humankind.

¹⁰ The whole message deals with the Jerusalem sanctuary and the Davidic monarchy.

¹¹ 2 Samuel 7:17. It is never easy to admit, 'I got it wrong.' How much more difficult if your job is to listen to God and give advice in his name! This must have been a humbling experience for Nathan.

¹² 2 Samuel 7:18. The narrator records, 'Then King David went in and sat before the Lord.' Although the temporary tent is not mentioned, it seems likely that this is what is referred to. The word translated 'sat' indicates (in Hebrew) that David sat back on his heels in a position for prayer.

¹³ 2 Samuel 7:18-29. David recorded his prayer in writing – as he did with other landmark events in his life. But from what we see of the man as portrayed in Scripture, there was more to his time alone before God than is recorded here. This was a period of intense intimacy with God.

¹⁴ 2 Samuel 7:18.

¹⁵ 2 Samuel 7:21.

¹⁶ 2 Samuel 7:25.

¹⁷ The clever use of the word 'house' in the prophetic word given by Nathan has been noted by others. A 'house' for God (2 Sam. 7:5) a 'house' (dynasty) for David (7:11) and 'a house for my Name' (7:13) draws out three promises. The first for the Jerusalem temple, the second for David's line that would run for four hundred years until 587 BC when the temple was destroyed and the dynasty ended. The 'house for my Name' was linked to the one whose throne would stand forever (7:13). This refers to God's long-range plan; a new Kingdom presided over by the Lord Jesus Christ.

¹⁸ Matthew 1:1-17. Matthew wrote his Gospel primarily for Jews and begins with a family tree of Jesus. This traces his family line (on Joseph's side) from Abraham, through David to Jesus. Jesus' credentials are spelt out as part of Matthew's case that he is the Christ, the Messiah sent by God.

[19] 1 Peter 2:4-10 gives a New Testament comment on this plan.

[20] Petersen, *Leap Over A Wall*, p161.

[21] Petersen, *Leap Over A Wall*, p161.

[22] Petersen, *Leap Over A Wall*, p165.

[23] Matthew 12:34 – 'For out of the overflow of the heart the mouth speaks.' What we say reveals what we feel in our hearts.

[24] 1 Chronicles 28:3. Something more of God's message to David is revealed here; 'God said to me, "You are not to build a house for my name because you are a warrior and have shed blood."'

[25] 2 Samuel 6:22. It is important not to confuse David's attitude here. 'I don't care what people think', can come from a proud, angry heart. David's contention is – if necessary – he would even become humiliated in his own estimation in order to honour and please God.

[26] 2 Samuel 7:19.

[27] 2 Samuel 7:1ff.

[28] 2 Corinthians 11:30. Paul, the Christian leader, discovered that there was a hidden strength in weakness.

[29] 2 Samuel 12:1ff – Nathan confronts David with the affair he was trying to cover up.

[30] Nathan's message is summarised, 'God showed Nathan that David's building plans for God would interfere with God's building plans for David.' Petersen, *Leap Over A Wall*, p160.

[31] 2 Samuel 7:19.

[32] Matthew 6:10.

18

Conquering

Listening to the story – 2 Samuel 8:1 – 10:19

This section of David's story reveals a period of expansion and conquest. The reason behind such growth is stated: 'The Lord gave David victory wherever he went.[1] God is fulfilling his promise to build David's kingdom and to defeat his enemies.[2]

David subdues the Philistines,[3] and then defeats the Moabites.[4] He executes two-thirds of their army, taxing the survivors.[5] Then he goes north, defeating Syrian king Hadadezer[6] and his allies, taking over their territory.[7] These victories bring great spoils of war into the royal treasury.[8] Through these victories, David pushes Israeli control north to the border of the River Euphrates.[9]

One king, Tou of Hamath, is relieved to learn that David had defeated Hadadezer as he has been fighting him. Tou offers David warm congratulations and costly gifts.[10] David dedicates these costly items to the Lord.[11] His victories continue: he defeats the Ammonites[12] and the Edomites.[13] These are not ventures of 'might and power'; David's victories ultimately come from the hand of God.[14]

David's reign is concerned with domestic affairs as well: 'David reigned over all Israel, doing what was just and right for all his people.[15] We are introduced to some of the key players in his administration: Joab – military commander, Jehoshaphat –

senior administrator, Zadok and Ahimelech – priests, Seraiah – secretary. Benaiah is also part of the palace team.[16] David's sons also play an important role as advisers.[17] The writer seems keen to point out that David's reign at this point is made up of conquests abroad, harmony at home and teamwork in the palace. It is an overall picture of a conquering king.

In the middle of this tale of David's growth and success comes the story of Mephibosheth, Jonathan's son.[18] It adds a human dimension to the story of conquest. David is not – yet – so absorbed with power that he loses sight of people. The all-powerful warrior king entertains the grandson of his greatest enemy at his table daily.[19] It is a powerful image of mercy and grace.

But David also experiences some set-backs – not everyone is pleased at his progress. The Ammonite king dies[20] and his son – Hanun – succeeds him. David recalls that Hanun's father showed him kindness when Saul was hunting for him and feels kindly disposed towards this new (possibly young) monarch.[21] He sends a diplomatic delegation to Hanun's palace, offering his condolences. Hanun's advisers convince him David's delegation is not genuine. It is an intelligence-gathering operation, assessing Ammonite strength.[22]

The king takes their advice and they humiliate David by abusing his messengers. They shave off part of their beards, cut away the lower part of their robes and send them back to Jerusalem.[23] News of this shameful treatment reaches David and he instructs his officials to stay away from Jerusalem until their beards have grown back.[24]

The Ammonites realise their actions will provoke a military response from David. Hiring in military muscle from surrounding states, they prepare for war.[25]

Joab, as David's military commander, marches out against the Ammonites – leading a massive force of troops.[26] The Ammonites defend their capital city while the hired troops draw up lines in open country. In response, Joab divides his soldiers. The crack troops he retains to face powerful Aramean mercenaries, while the less experienced are placed under the command of his brother Abishai with orders to attack the

Ammonite defenders. Both agree to monitor the course of the battle and – if necessary – to aid the other.[27]

Joab concludes his orders with a call of faith in the power of Yahweh to deliver them: 'Be strong and let us fight bravely for our people and the cities of our God. The Lord will do what is good in his sight.'[28]

What transpired is quite remarkable. The hired Arameans run away and the Ammonites withdraw into the city, pulling up the drawbridge. No-one wants to fight. Joab makes the decision to return to Jerusalem – at least for now.[29] But the fleeing Arameans decide to continue. Regrouping, they call for reinforcements, determined this time to stand and fight. David and his army meet them on the east side of the Jordan at Helam,[30] inflicting a heavy defeat on the Arameans.[31] They decide any further political or military support for the Ammonites is not worth it.[32]

The defeat has further political implications as those kings that were subservient to the Arameans transfer their allegiance to David.[33] His power across the region is consolidated further. This period in David's reign records conquest after conquest. Within the history of Israel these were days that would go down as memorable. As Alan Redpath remarks,

> Significantly, it was for the first and almost the last time in history up to now that the people of God possessed the whole territory which God's covenant with Abraham said that they should have. Back when Abraham did not possess an inch of the land, God said, 'Unto thy seed have I given this land, from the river of Egypt unto the Great River, the river Euphrates.' (Genesis 15:18).[34]

David takes territory for God. Significantly, that only occurs because 'the Lord gave David victory wherever he went.' God is working out his purposes through David's life.

Learning from the story

There are some sharp insights on life contained within these chapters. For example, we are reminded of the wisdom of

kindness and the folly of unkindness. David, in his treatment
of Mephibosheth, provides a glimpse of the grace of God in
Jesus.[35] But such a touching incident is countered by an act of
great folly. Through listening to bad advice, Hanun made a
foolish decision that had serious implications.[36]

When faced with similar choices we should choose the path
marked kindness. The most important lesson is found in
David's resolute determination to press on for the best that
God has for him. It would have been easy for him to have
stayed in Jerusalem, opting for a quiet life.[37] But David busied
himself about God's business.

This is best seen in a psalm he wrote at this period in his life,
Psalm 60.[38] It gives insights into David's inner life. The meditation breaks into three parts:

● Israel's predicament (vv1-4)
● God's promise (vv5-8)
● David's prayer (vv9-12)

Israel's predicament – vv1-4

David paints a picture of a rejected nation, under God's judgement. They have been through 'desperate times', the dark
days of Saul's reign, the momentous defeat against the
Philistines and the calamity of division. But there is hope that
God will save his chosen people, who are in desperate need.[39]

God's promise – vv5-8

God speaks prophetically through David's composition and
reveals his sovereign power. All the nations are under his control. Succoth (east of Jordan) and Shechem (west of it) were
places where Jacob pitched camp when he returned from
exile.[40] Gilead, Manasseh, Ephraim and Judah refer to territo-
ries taken by Israel when the tribes entered the Promised
Land.

If the tribes of Ephraim and Judah were a helmet and scep-
tre to the Lord, then Moab is a mere bucket, Edom a slave and

Philistia a defeated foe.[41] The overall picture is the sovereignty
of an Almighty God. Ultimately in the affairs of humankind –
heaven rules.

David's prayer – vv9-12

His petition is heartfelt:

> Give us aid against the enemy,
> for the help of man is worthless.
> With God we shall gain the victory,
> and he will trample down our enemies.[42]

In this situation of national need, David turns God's promise
into prayer. David then goes out to fight, and the stunning victories that follow are a direct result of prayer. Truly, 'The Lord
gave David victory wherever he went.'[43] For those who seek to
follow Christ, David offers us a picture of the life of faith. God
has fresh ground for us to take and yet – like David – we face
the temptation to live at ease.

The decision to follow Christ wholeheartedly is akin to
handing over the title deeds of your life and inviting him in to
take possession. Room by room he moves around, clearing out
the junk and unwanted furniture, redecorating and cleaning
the place up. The process of growth is one of gradual change
as we submit our lives more and more to the control of Jesus.
But some of us are content to let him into the entrance hall and
no further. There are rooms that are locked and bolted. We put
a limit on what God wants to accomplish in and through us.
David's situation underlines the importance of not settling for
less than the best.

The challenge that David poses is one of conquest. Are we
content to remain in possession of part of what God has for us
– or do we want the full extent of the territory? Perhaps Psalm
60 is a good starting point for those who long to enter into
what it means to be 'more than conquerors'.[44]

The following true story was told by a church leader. When
he was sixteen years old, he and his younger cousins went to

stay on their grandfather's farm. They were keen to get out and let off steam. Initially the grandfather was reluctant to let them roam around unsupervised – but they begged and pleaded until he gave way. He agreed, but on one strict condition – they must stay out all day and under no circumstances come back to the house. Everyone agreed and set off. After a couple of hours of tackling some small chores and generally playing around, the children began to get tired and bored. It was a hot, sticky day and several wanted to go back to the farmhouse. But their cousin refused. 'Grandad said stay!' he told them.

By lunchtime they had eaten all their food supplies and were thoroughly irritated. They wanted to do something else, so they asked their eldest cousin if they could go back to the house. 'No,' he replied firmly.

By mid-afternoon, large storm clouds loomed in the sky. Some of the younger ones began to cry. 'Please can we go back?' they begged. Their cousin remained resolute. Eventually, around five o'clock he led them back to the farmhouse for some welcome baths and a good meal. Their grandfather congratulated them on their achievement and explained why he had wanted them to stay out all day.

> This farm has been successful through the years for one reason. We have stayed in the field when we felt like coming in. We did what needed to be done even when we wanted to quit. I wanted you kids to have the satisfying experience of staying with something through the day.

They all learned a lasting lesson from that experience and the oldest cousin, recounting the story years later as a Christian leader, remarked on its influence on his life.[45]

The willingness to 'stay in the field' is the spirit that lay behind David's conquests. God granted him victory and taught him many lessons along the way. But the victories of God didn't happen while David sat in his palace composing psalms. He had to get out into the field and be willing to stay there when the battle was tough.

Of such stuff conquerors are made.

1. 2 Samuel 8:6, 14.
2. The Lord spelt out this promise to David in 2 Samuel 7:8-11.
3. 2 Samuel 8:1. Metheg Ammah may be a reference to the famous Philistine city of Gath (1 Chr. 18:1).
4. 2 Samuel 8:2.
5. Such a harsh reaction suggests the Moabites had threatened Israel's security. In earlier times there had been such a good relationship between David and the Moabites, he had sent his parents to Moab (1 Sam. 22:3-4).
6. 2 Samuel 8:3-4
7. 2 Samuel 8:5-6.
8. 2 Samuel 8:7-8.
9. 2 Samuel 8:3
10. 2 Samuel 8:9-10.
11. David had not lost sight of his dream of a temple for the Lord. Later these spoils of war would be used to make his dream come true (2 Chr. 5:1).
12. 2 Samuel 8:1.2
13. 2 Samuel 8:13-14.
14. Zechariah 4:6: Zerubbabel is told emphatically, 'Not by might nor by power, but by my Spirit says the Lord Almighty.' David has learned the same principle of godly authority.
15. 2 Samuel 8:15.
16. 2 Samuel 8:16-18.
17. 2 Samuel 8:18. The Hebrew word translated 'royal advisers' (NIV) means 'priests', indicating there may well have been a religious aspect to their duties involving prayer and worship.
18. See chapter 4.
19. 2 Samuel 9:13.
20. 2 Samuel 10:1.
21. We can only assume that this was what David meant when he speaks of Nahash's kindness to him. 1 Samuel 11:1ff records a fierce battle between Saul and Nahash where the Ammonites were heavily defeated. Perhaps this made him an ally for David when Saul sought to kill him.
22. David had made a reputation for himself by his military conquests and the Ammonite advisers had every reason to be wary of a strong, united Israel on their border. The reference in 2 Samuel

8:12 to David subduing the Ammonites may refer to the events of chapter 10 – but it may be a reference to an earlier period when David defeated the Ammonite army. If so, the actions of Hanun's advisers are more understandable.

[23] This was designed to create maximum humiliation not only for David's officials – but for David himself.

[24] 2 Samuel 10:5. The men are told to wait in Jericho for their beards to grow back.

[25] 2 Samuel 10:6 mentions a total of 33,000 hired troops. The ability to raise such numbers in a short space of time begs the question; 'Were the Ammonites looking for a fight?'

[26] 2 Samuel 10:7: the narrator points out that 'David sent Joab out with the entire army of fighting men.' A serious insult demanded a strong response.

[27] 2 Samuel 10:9-11. Joab's tactics suggest this Ammonite alliance was a credible force which demanded careful attention.

[28] 2 Samuel 10:12.

[29] The incidents of chapter 10 set the context for the events of subsequent chapters. David's adultery and his attempt to cover it up with the murder of Uriah took place during the battle against the Ammonites (2 Sam. 11:1ff).

[30] 2 Samuel 10:15-17. Perhaps it was sheer force of numbers that made them withdraw initially. Reinforced with troops from 'beyond the River' (v16) (i.e. the Euphrates) they were more confident to face Israel.

[31] 2 Samuel 10:18. The Arameans lost over 40,000 soldiers and charioteers, their senior commander was killed and they were left diminished in power.

[32] 2 Samuel 10:19. The Arameans decide to tear up their agreement with the Ammonites. The royal advisers to Hanun gambled and lost.

[33] 2 Samuel 11:19. This defeat greatly weakened the hold of Aram as their vassals switched to David. This would mean greater revenue, more power and better security for Israel.

[34] Redpath, *The Making of A Man of God*, p178

[35] 2 Samuel 9:1ff. Many have seen in this touching story a picture of God's grace to us through the Lord Jesus Christ. We are disabled by sin, counted as God's enemies, deserving of punishment. Yet in

love he seeks us out and sits us at his table and calls us his children. Even the name of the place where he is living in hiding is significant. 'Lo Debar' (v4) means, 'the place of no pasture'.

[36] 2 Samuel 10:1ff.

[37] David was to fall prey to this temptation soon (2 Sam. 11:1ff).

[38] The superscription at the head of Psalm 60 places it within the events described in 2 Samuel 8.

[39] Some see a reference to the judgement of God through the attack by Edom. 'Psalm 60 implies an Edomite invasion which was a real threat, and a punishment, perhaps for a war God had not sanctioned.' M. Wilcock, *The Message of Psalms 1-72*, The Bible Speaks Today Series (Leicester: IVP, 2001), p215-6.

[40] Genesis 33:17ff.

[41] 'Moab is my washbasin' (Ps. 60:8) has puzzled many. The point is that God is all powerful and even the strongest nation can be used by him to accomplish his will.

[42] Psalm 60:11-12.

[43] 2 Samuel 8:6, 14.

[44] Romans 8:37.

[45] Dr John Corts, formerly President of the Billy Graham Organisation. The story is adapted from the *Focus on the Family Newsheet*, May 2002. Focus on the Family, Colorado Springs, CO 80995, USA.

19

Failure

Listening to the story – 2 Samuel 11:1 – 12:25

The Bible never hides the failures of its heroes. This episode charts both David's moral and spiritual failure and, more importantly, how he found his way back. We learn from both sides.

The siege of Rabbah resumes in the spring – but for some reason David chooses to stay back in Jerusalem.[1] Joab commands the Israelite army

One night David is unable to sleep and strolls around the palace roof. He spots a beautiful woman taking a bath in her house – and immediately falls head over heels in lust. David discovers the woman's name is Bathsheba and she is married to one of his own fighting men – Uriah – a Hittite. Although a foreigner, he is well-integrated into the life and religion of Israel.[2] David sends messengers to invite this beautiful woman to the palace and she responds. They meet at the palace and the two of them end up having sex.

Bathsheba returns home and there appears to be no further contact[3] until she sends the king a message – 'I'm pregnant!'[4]

Unless something happens quickly the affair will become public knowledge, causing considerable embarrassment to the king. The scandal could destabilise the nation, spiritually and politically. The penalty for adultery in Israel is death and

David is the nation's most senior judge. This could cause a national crisis.

David orders Joab to send Uriah back from the front-line with a campaign update.[5] Uriah returns with his report. David assumes that Uriah will go home for the night and take the opportunity to make love to his wife, Bathsheba. But Uriah prefers to sleep with the royal servants in the palace.[6]

The next morning David learns his plan has failed. Uriah pleads solidarity with Commander Joab and his officers, camped in open fields. How can Uriah enjoy the finer things of life while they are a long way from the comforts of home?

Persuading Uriah to stay on, David gets Uriah drunk to weaken his resolve. But once again, Uriah opts for the coldness of the palace floor.[7]

David realises that his cover-up plan won't work. He decides Uriah must die. David writes a note to his commander, Joab, that Uriah carries, telling Joab to place Uriah at the heart of the fighting and then abandon him: 'so that he will be struck down and die.'[8]

At the earliest opportunity, Joab places Uriah up against the strongest Ammonite soldiers. These defenders break out of the city, successfully attacking some Israeli troops. Uriah the Hittite is one of those who dies.[9]

Joab sends a report of the incident back to Jerusalem. Realising the report of deaths may provoke David's anger,[10] Joab includes the words, 'Your servant Uriah the Hittite is dead.'[11] The messenger brings his report to David[12] who sympathises with Joab's loss and sends back a message of encouragement.[13]

After a respectful period of mourning, David marries Bathsheba hastily. The affair has been successfully covered up. Those who could do their sums would realise what had happened[14] but the general public didn't know the whole story and the royal image was secure. But Heaven had noticed: 'The thing David had done displeased the Lord.'[15]

After David and Bathsheba's son was born, Nathan[16] tells the king a shocking story of gross injustice.[17] Two men lived in the same town – one rich, the other poor. The rich man owned a huge number of sheep and cattle but the poor man had one ewe lamb that was treated like one of the family. A traveller visited the rich man and he entertained him to a meal. But instead of choosing an animal from his extensive stock, he stole the poor man's lamb and cooked it.

David is furious, determined that the rich man should not go unpunished. He deserves death and will be made to compensate his neighbour. David demands to know his name.

Nathan utters four words. 'You are the man!'[18] He delivers God's verdict on the case that David has tried to bury:[19]

- God placed him on the throne and gave everything of Saul's house into his control[20]
- The Lord would have given David even more than all that he has already placed into his hands[21]
- David has despised the word of the Lord – shown by his murderous actions[22]
- Because David killed Uriah with the sword – violence will never be removed from David's house (or line)[23]
- David's actions showed he despises the Lord, Yahweh[24]
- The consequence of David's sin is that calamity will come upon his family – and his punishment known to all[25]

David's actions were secretive, but the Lord will deal with him publicly for his sin. Nathan tackled the hardest job of his life in acting as God's messenger to David that day.[26]

David's response is immediate and real. Without hesitation, he declares, 'I have sinned against the Lord.'[27] Nathan tells David that his sin has been forgiven – but the judgement of God will still be carried out. The child born to David and Bathsheba will die.[28] The baby becomes ill that night. David immediately fasts and prays intensely. For a week, the child hovers between life and death and David keeps up his vigil of prayer, refusing to get up or to eat.[29]

At the end of the week the baby dies and David's closest advisers are petrified over what the king will do when he knows. No-one wants to tell him as they genuinely believe he might even attempt suicide in grief.[30] But when David learns the sad news, he immediately reverts to normality, washing, dressing and worshipping in the tent of the Ark. He then returns to the palace to eat some food for the first time in a week.[31]

David's advisers are puzzled at his bizarre behaviour and ask him why he is acting against the norm.[32] The king explains he has been interceding for the child's life but now accepts that this is not to be.[33] He must now get on with the rest of his life.

The narrator draws this dark episode to a close with a cameo of grace. David and Bathsheba find comfort in each other. Doubtless they both wish they could undo their actions. God graciously gives them another son, Solomon. It is a special name for a special child,[34] a name given by the Lord himself through a message delivered by Nathan.[35]

Of this child, Solomon, Scripture records, 'The Lord loved him.'[36]

Learning from the story

This stark episode reveals two important truths. They can be summed up in two phrases:

- Following the way down
- Finding the way back up again

Following the way down

The Bible doesn't go into great detail about David's failure. It leaves much unsaid. But David's failure puts up some large warnings. We tread similar ground to David every day of our lives.

Three words summarise a downward path that David had been following for some time.

- Compromised
- Comfortable
- Complacent

Compromised

Few people wake up in the morning and say, 'Today I will commit adultery.' It is usually a gradual slide. When David began to consolidate the kingdom and establish himself in his new capital, Jerusalem, he let his standards slip.[37] By taking new wives and concubines he was simply doing what everyone expected of a potentate. It encouraged an appetite that David needed to control, adding momentum to a temptation that gripped David on the palace roof later.

If we want to learn from David's personal failure, then it is worth reflecting on this question. Are there areas of my life where I am letting my defences slip?

Comfortable

The story's opening statement reveals the state of David's life.[38] He sent Joab to lead the army when he should have gone himself. Life was comfortable for David: he didn't need to prove himself. But this was dangerous because comfort produced spiritual lethargy. David – the man of passion and energy for God – found his passion and energy diverted in other directions.

David's collapse poses an important question. Am I pursuing God – and all he has for me – with eagerness?

Complacent

David felt secure in Jerusalem. His enemies were subdued, life was good to him. But he had begun to forget who had put him there. David's worship life began to grow cold. We can see the eroding effects of complacency in his actions.

David should have been out with the army, he shouldn't have taken a second, third and fourth look at Bathsheba. He shouldn't have enquired about her, he shouldn't have invited her to the palace, he shouldn't have gone to bed with her. He shouldn't have tried to cover up, he shouldn't have tried to deceive Uriah, he shouldn't have arranged to have the loyal soldier killed.

The list is a long one and we can check the boxes along the way. 'It could never happen to me', are dangerous words to utter, because they are born of pride and rooted in naiveté. We can trace complacency in David with ease – but what of our own lives? We face another personal question:

Am I drifting?

Finding the way back up again

Fortunately, David's heart was more tender than Saul's and his repentance was genuine.[39] The famous Psalm 51 reflects the anguish David faced as his sin was exposed. It has been a help to countless thousands over the generations because it so captures what a broken and contrite heart looks, sounds and feels like.

From David's recovery we note some important things about his repentance.

Its speed

David immediately owned up to what he had done when confronted by Nathan. There was no half-hearted admission– he pleaded guilty.

Its focus

There is a sharp understanding that primarily David has offended the Lord. Both the narrative and the psalm make this clear.[40] Our sins affect others – but the greatest offence is to the God who made us for better things.

Its depth

David's behaviour when the baby battled for life tells us much about the reality of his penitence. These are the actions of a man deeply convicted and challenged about what he had done.

Its results

David found forgiveness because God is a God of love. But he had to live with the disastrous consequences of his actions because God is a God of justice too.

If David's failure offers us warning signs dealing with compromise, comfort and complacency, then his repentance provides an example of finding the way back.

I have never forgotten a conversation with a police detective during the course of a trial. The prisoner, who faced a serious charge, was sentenced and I visited him before he was taken away. As I left, I mentioned the prisoner showed signs of remorse. The policeman commented, 'I have learned there are two types of "sorry". Most say, "I'm sorry I got caught"; few ever mean "I'm sorry I ever did it."'

That policeman showed great understanding of the New Testament verse that says, 'Godly sorrow brings repentance that leads to salvation and leaves no regret, but worldly sorrow brings death.'[41] David shows what godly sorrow looks like. At the very pinnacle of his God-given power, he falls into sin and the consequences devastate the rest of his life. This deserves sober reflection and serious attention to the state of our own hearts.

It has been pointed out that the use of the word 'send' in the narrative is significant.[42] It is used to indicate David's wrong use of power and his decline into using people to achieve his own ends. David slides into 'sending' because he had forgotten that he was himself 'sent' by the Lord.

David stopped living under God's power and began to exercise his own.

At which point, it always starts to go wrong.

---

[1] 2 Samuel 10:14. Joab led the attack on the Ammonites but withdrew to Jerusalem. It seems that the siege of Rabbah (modern-day Amman in Jordan) resumed the following spring.

[2] Although he was a Hittite, Uriah's name means 'Yahweh is my Light' which indicates faith in Israel's God on his part or on the part of his parents.

3 Was this no more than a one-night stand? It seems to be so as the next contact between them is initiated by Bathsheba, leaving long enough for her to miss her period and conclude she is pregnant.

4 2 Samuel 11:4. The reference to Bathsheba having 'purified herself from her uncleanness' means she had just finished menstruating. Therefore, as David was the only person she had intercourse with between her periods, he must be the father.

5 2 Samuel 11:6ff. Regular reports would be sent to the king about the progress of the siege. David is using Uriah as the messenger. This suggests that Uriah was possibly more than just a foot soldier – perhaps an officer..

6 Some will see here the actions of a loyal servant. Uriah's refusal to enjoy personal comfort is explained as an act of devotion to the king and his interests (2 Sam. 11:11). It is equally possible that all was not as it should be in his own marriage. Others suggest that men at war took an oath to abstain from sexual relations as a sign of their consecration (1 Sam. 21:4-5).

7 2 Samuel 1:12-13.

8 2 Samuel 11:15.

9 Here is a commander instructed by his Commander-in-Chief deliberately to let innocent men die with Uriah, in order to cover up his dishonourable actions.

10 2 Samuel 11:18-21. Joab anticipates the king's anger at a basic military blunder, allowing soldiers to get too close to the wall in a siege situation.

11 2 Samuel 11:21.

12 2 Samuel 11:22-24. Only Joab and David understood the significance of the message about Uriah's death.

13 2 Samuel 11:25. There is something cynical about David's use of the phrase: 'Don't let this upset you, the sword devours one as well as another.' Sin truly makes you deaf, blind – and daft.

14 As with any royal court, gossip would be rife. But they had (in modern terms) 'managed to keep the story out of the tabloids'. David's primary concern was image – not morality.

15 2 Samuel 11:27.

16 2 Samuel 12:1ff.

17 2 Samuel 12:1-4. David believed this was a genuine case-study he was hearing which accounts for his strong desire to

discover who the guilty man is (vv5-6) and to have him punished.

[18] 2 Samuel 12:7.

[19] 2 Samuel 12:7-12. The impact of this short, sharp exposé must have been enormous, not only on David but on all who heard it.

[20] 2 Samuel 12:7-8 'I gave your master's house to you, and your master's wives into your arms ...' is a reference to the house of Saul (including his harem) passing into David's hands.

[21] 2 Samuel 12:8. God had brought David a long way (2 Sam. 7:18) – and he had even more in store for this favoured man. But David had forfeited that.

[22] 2 Samuel 12:9.

[23] 2 Samuel 12:9-10.

[24] 2 Samuel 12:14. David's sin is seen as a personal affront to the Lord. This powerful indictment helps us understand the depth of David's confession in Psalm 51:4: 'Against you, you only, have I sinned and done what is evil in your sight.'

[25] 2 Samuel 12:11-12. The awful consequence of David's sin is that his own family would be divided and his own wives violated by someone close to him.

[26] Petersen, *Leap Over A Wall*, p185, comments; 'This is what preachers are for, to bring us into focus in the story. The art of preaching is to somehow or other get around our third-person defences and compel a second- person recognition, which enables a first-person response.'

[27] 2 Samuel 12:13. David's swift and honest response brings an immediate word of forgiveness from God. But the consequences of his sin are not avoided.

[28] 2 Samuel 12:13-14. Two things stand out from Nathan's reply. First, the immediate removal of David's sin. It is 'taken away' (v13) implying a complete cleansing (see Ps. 103:11-13). Secondly, David's sin has become known to 'the enemies of the Lord' (v14) and they hold both him and the Lord in utter contempt. David's credibility as a man after God's heart had been tarnished beyond measure. It is a sobering thought that while we may find forgiveness in an instant, it takes a long time to recover credibility.

[29] 2 Samuel 12:15-18.

[30] 2 Samuel 12:18. David's actions raised concern within the palace.

³¹ 2 Samuel 12:19-20.

³² 2 Samuel 12:21. The accepted practice would be for mourning to begin at the death of a person. Deep grief may well include the sort of things David had done in his distress, seeking solitude, fasting and prayer. But he had done this before the child died.

³³ 2 Samuel 12:23.

³⁴ The name Solomon (or 'Jedidiah') means 'beloved of the Lord'.

³⁵ 2 Samuel 12:25.

³⁶ 2 Samuel 12:24.

³⁷ 2 Samuel 5:13ff tells us David took more wives and concubines. See chapter 15, footnote 11.

³⁸ 2 Samuel 11:1ff.

³⁹ It is interesting to contrast Saul's declaration, 'I have sinned', with David's (1 Sam. 15:24ff). Saul's confession was not accepted by God as genuine, reminding us that heart response is what God seeks.

⁴⁰ Compare 2 Samuel 12:13 with Psalm 51:4. David had sinned against a list of people – including himself. But the major issue was with the Lord – the One to whom we are all ultimately accountable.

⁴¹ 2 Corinthians 7:10.

⁴² Petersen, *Leap Over A Wall*, p183ff

20

Divided

Listening to the story – 2 Samuel 13:1 – 14:33

Actions have consequences. David has already learned that following his affair with Bathsheba. Time has passed[1] but the implications of his actions linger on – not least within his own extended family. This leads to the stormiest period of David's reign, in which he seems to move backwards so far as God's purpose for his life is concerned.

David has several wives and concubines who have borne him a large number of children. The eldest of his sons is Amnon and the third son is Absalom.[2] Absalom has a sister, Tamar and Amnon – her half brother – is totally besotted by her. His desire becomes an obsession that begins to affect his health.[3] Amnon has a cousin, Jonadab, who suggests Amnon should feign serious illness. When David visits and asks what can be done to help, then Amnon should ask for Tamar to prepare some food for him. Jonadab is simply offering Amnon a chance to get Tamar alone.[4]

Amnon agrees and Tamar is sent to prepare him a meal. She serves it to him but he refuses to eat until everyone leaves the room. Feigning weakness, he asks her to bring the food into the bedroom. Tamar complies, but as she serves the meal Amnon grabs her and seeks to seduce her.[5]

Tamar tries to hold him off and pleads for him to think about his actions. In her desperation she even urges him to speak to David and seek permission for them to marry.[6] Amnon ignores her pleas and brutally rapes her.

Suddenly Amnon's mood changes. His lust satiated, his heart is turned to loathing.[7]

Tamar refuses to go at first so he has her thrown out. Covered with grief and shame, Tamar puts on the clothes of mourning usually worn when someone has been bereaved.[8]

Her brother Absalom discovers what has happened and offers her comfort of sorts. David hears the news eventually and is filled with anger. But neither of them takes any action. On Absalom's part, he acts as if Amnon doesn't even exist.[9] The matter is hushed up and a veil of family secrecy is drawn around the incident.[10] Like so many families, this royal household decides to play 'Let's Pretend'.

Two years pass before Absalom's revenge is executed. He decides to throw a party for his sheep-shearers and includes the royal family in his invitation list. King David politely declines but gives his blessing for the celebrations to go ahead in his absence.[11] Absalom ensures that all David's sons (his own brothers and half-brothers) are brought along. Specifically, he includes Amnon in his guest list which causes David to raise a question; why is Amnon suddenly back in favour with Absalom?[12] No clear answer is offered but Absalom stresses that Amnon is warmly invited to attend and so – with the king's permission – he joins the royal party.

With the party in full swing – and Amnon full of wine – at a prearranged signal, Absalom orders his men into action and they cut Amnon down in cold blood. In the ensuing panic, David's other sons flee for their lives, fearing that a palace coup has been launched.[13]

The news that reaches David at first is that all the royal princes have been butchered. Understandably, he and his officials react with great grief. Then Jonadab appears, telling David that Absalom has only killed Amnon – to avenge his sister's honour.[14] Eventually a traumatised group of princes return to the royal palace. The capital is buzzing with rumours in every quarter.[15]

Absalom seeks refuge with his mother's family in Geshur[16] and a heartbroken David mourns deeply for the loss of two sons. The narrator suggests that David – in some measure at least – comes to terms with Amnon's murder, yet remains in a constant state of grief for his son Absalom.[17]

Joab is a loyal servant and friend to David, serving as his military commander.[18] He has been with David in various seasons of his life and is concerned to see his uncle, friend and master consumed by grief. Joab hatches a plan that he hopes will ultimately bring some reconciliation between David and Absalom. It involves a woman who possesses some special gifting, living in Tekoa.[19] Joab gives her strict instructions about her dress, demeanour and the story she is to tell King David.

The woman dresses in deep mourning and seeks an audience with the king on an urgent matter of justice. She tells David that she is a widow with two sons. They got into a fight and one killed the other. Now her family are seeking blood revenge for the slain brother, demanding she hands over her surviving son to be executed. The woman's plight is plain; her surviving son is the only heir: 'They would put out the only burning coal I have left, leaving my husband neither name nor descendant on the face of the earth.'[20]

King David promises he will consider her case and sends her home. But the woman persists, claiming that she and her family will bear any guilt in the matter.[21] David tells her to refer anyone to him who raises with her the question of her fugitive son being brought to justice. The woman asks David to invoke an oath in the name of Yahweh against anyone who would pursue her son to death. David gives her an assurance in the name of Yahweh that her son will not be harmed.[22]

The anonymous woman presses her case to its climax. If the king is able to make a decree in the case of her surviving son that will grant him immunity from prosecution, why can't he find it in his heart to forgive and restore Absalom? She makes a remarkable statement about the merciful kindness of God: 'Like water spilled on the ground, which cannot be recovered, so we must die. But God does not take away life; instead he devises ways so that a banished person may not remain estranged from him.'[23] The woman pleads for justice for her son – and justice, too, for the king's son, Absalom. In so doing she honours David and seeks God's blessing on his life.[24]

David spots the hand of Joab in this and challenges the woman to tell him the truth. She admits that Joab has put her up to this but points out that his motives are both true and clear.[25]

Joab's efforts (and we suspect his prayers as well) bear fruit and David agrees to allow Absalom back home. Joab sets off with the good news that Absalom can return to Jerusalem. But David stipulates Absalom may return but will not be allowed into the king's presence.[26]

Absalom had four children – three sons and a daughter. Significantly, when his little girl is born he names her Tamar after his sister whose life had been so cruelly crushed. She grows into a very beautiful woman.[27]

Absalom lives in this state of internal banishment for a period of two years. During this time, he doesn't see his father David face to face. Eventually, Absalom sends for Joab in the hope that he can reintroduce him to the royal court. After all, Joab had been the skilful negotiator who had brought him back to Jerusalem; perhaps he could act as Absalom's emissary to his father David?

Joab refuses all invitations even to meet with Absalom. Perhaps David had laid this down as a precondition of allowing his fugitive son back to the capital? So impatient Absalom orders his men to set fire to one of Joab's fields, adjoining his own property. Joab comes to survey the damage and is told that Absalom's men deliberately started the fire, so he makes his way to confront him. Absalom explains he can no longer continue living in Jerusalem yet banished from his father's presence. He throws out a bold challenge: 'I want to see the king's face, and if I am guilty of anything, let him put me to death.'[28]

Joab intercedes again with David on Absalom's behalf. The king agrees to have Absalom back into the royal court. The episode ends with the poignant phrase: 'And the king kissed Absalom.'[29]

David and Absalom are reconciled – at least on the surface. But what lies beneath will, in the long run, prove to be lethal.

Learning from the story

These events in David's life directly fulfil the word of the Lord through Nathan.[30] God had forgiven David but he lived with the implications of his sins. His family was affected by his affair and the attempt to cover it up through murdering Bathsheba's husband, Uriah. This reminds us of Paul's words in the New Testament: 'Do not be deceived: God cannot be mocked. A man reaps what he sows.'[31]

This tale involves a number of characters and from each we learn something important about life that can be summarised in one word.

- Amnon – Appetites
- Tamar – Brokenness
- David – Weakness
- Absalom – Revenge
- Joab – Peacemaking

Amnon – Appetites

God made us with appetites for food, water, sleep and sex. But uncontrolled appetites are dangerous because, left unchecked, they can distort and ultimately destroy. Amnon is a powerful example of this. He fell head over heels for a woman and his common sense fled. He let his feelings get out of control, raping her and irreparably wrecking her life.

The Holy Spirit is in the fruit production business. His one fruit comes in nine flavours, one of which is simply described as self-control.[32] All our appetites need to be subject to his control. Growing in faith as disciples of Christ involves allowing God to teach us to keep our appetites in check. It is a learning process – and one where we will make mistakes and, at times, fail. But as far as appetites are concerned, we want to be running them rather than them running us.

Tamar – Brokenness

The narrator paints a tragic portrait of Tamar. Having been used and abused by her half-brother, she ends up a broken, lonely woman. 'And Tamar lived in her brother Absalom's house, a desolate woman.'[33] Innocent people are ruined by others' greed and selfishness. We do not know what happened to Tamar, but custom would dictate that she could not marry or have children but would live with the scars of Amnon's moment of passion. She found love and acceptance in her brother's house and his decision to name his daughter after her perhaps was part of her healing.

Tamar reminds us that we are surrounded by the victims of sin and injustice. Is there hope for the Tamars of our world? According to the Bible the answer is a 'Yes!' The death of Jesus on the cross is able to deal with the penalty of sin and also its power. The prophet Isaiah expresses it thus,

> But he (Jesus) was pierced for our transgressions,
> he was crushed for our iniquities;
> the punishment that brought us peace was upon him,
> and by his wounds we are healed.[34]

We can find healing and freedom through the cross of Christ. His blood poured out at the cross has no limits to its power and if we come with openness and faith we can find release from all the wrongs that have been done to us.

I spoke once to a woman who had known great pain in her life that had led to a prolonged period of depression and breakdown. Mercifully, she was offered professional help. Her counsellor, a Christian psychiatrist, skilfully helped her begin to put the pieces back together again. She decided to climb out of her pit of personal pain and look at the world from a new place. God had given her the freedom to choose. And she was choosing to be free.

That is a message of hope for all Tamars.

David – Weakness

Whatever happened to the clear-sighted, courageous warrior king? Here we see a weak and compromised ruler who can't even keep his family together. He had fallen in lust and now his eldest son Amnon follows suit. David ordered Uriah's murder. Absalom does the same to Amnon. Both of these men were products of marriages of convenience that the Lord had never commanded.[35] David looks weak and worn out.

David's weakness is further highlighted by two things. First, he fails to deal with Amnon's sin. His own daughter has been violated and yet David does nothing. Had he lost the moral high ground with his family and court? Did he want to avoid a public scandal?

Whatever his reasons, it was an appalling decision.

Secondly, his treatment of Absalom lacks any sense of grace. When he is persuaded to allow Absalom back to Jerusalem after a period of three years, he refuses to see him. His love was sentimental – real love is tough. Absalom needed a father. His arrogance needed challenging, his talent needed harnessing – and his sin needed forgiving.

David kissed his son – but he did it two years too late. If only he had dealt out the grace which he himself had been dealt![36]

Absalom – Revenge

Many would sympathise with Absalom in his actions. His sister had been raped, his father was incapable of dealing with the situation and Amnon seemed to be getting away with it. If we get our moral guidance from the soaps or *Big Brother*,[37] then Absalom may be seen as an altogether decent man with his family's interests at heart.

But if we draw our ideas of right and wrong from God, we conclude that Absalom was taking the law into his own hands. Moreover, we learn that he had been planning his revenge for a long time.[38] He carried out his plan to murder Amnon as soon as he could.

'Two wrongs don't make a right.' It is good to be passionate about justice and to fight for it to prevail. But revenge is out of the question for the man or woman who wants to go God's way.

A new life demands a new lifestyle.[39]

Joab – Peacemaking

According to Jesus, 'Blessed are the peacemakers, for they will be called sons of God.'[40] God's family business is reconciliation. As the anonymous wise woman from Tekoa declared, God always seeks to find a way back for lost people.[41] Whenever we engage in seeking to bring estranged people back together, we become involved in God-work.

Joab took a great risk in broaching the matter with David on two occasions. He could have opted for the quiet life but two things motivated him. First, concern for his friend. He was close enough to David to read his heart,[42] the mark of close friendship. Joab went beyond empathy and embraced involvement. He could see that David longed to put things right with Absalom so he did what he could. It didn't work out. But that was down to David's own failure. Joab did what he could out of a good motive of concern for his friend.

But secondly, Joab was driven by a commitment to the kingdom. He could see the potential danger in Absalom remaining estranged from David. The stability of the kingdom and the welfare of the nation was at stake. Israel was enjoying a sustained period of peace and prosperity. Joab could see that this situation was dangerous.

Thank God for friends who are willing to be peacemakers and retain a vision of our own best interests and the bigger picture of the Kingdom of God. Here is a much needed yet often neglected ministry within the Body of Christ – the peacemakers. May we aspire to such a role, and carry on the family business.

The story has much to say to us about controlling our appetites, finding healing for our brokenness, challenging our weaknesses, rejecting revenge and pursuing peacemaking.

May they be lessons we learn well.

1   The narrator introduces this episode with the words: 'In the course of time …' (2 Sam.13:1). This indicates life has moved on for David.

2   2 Samuel 3:2-3. They were both born during David's time in Hebron. Amnon's mother was Ahinoam from Jezreel and Absalom's mother was Maacah, the daughter of the king of Geshur.

3   2 Samuel 13:2. Amnon had made overtures to Tamar that she had either not noticed or had chosen to ignore.

4   It would have been hard in the normal course of events for Amnon to have spent time alone with Tamar.

5   2 Samuel 13:11. Whoever said sin is stupid was quite right. How could Amnon ever imagine that his approach would be remotely attractive to Tamar? Here is a man ruled by his appetites.

6   According to Mosaic Law, marriage between a half-brother and sister was not permitted (see Lev. 18:11). Perhaps Tamar was seeking to defuse a dangerous situation. On the other hand, she may have been genuinely inviting Amnon to see if marriage might be permitted.

7   2 Samuel 13:15 makes for sad reading, 'Then Amnon hated her with intense hatred. In fact, he hated her more than he had loved her.'

8   2 Samuel 13:19. Not only has Tamar suffered a violent rape by someone in her family circle, she knows that no-one else will marry her. The stigma will live with her for the rest of her life. As the narrator records, 'And Tamar lived in her brother Absalom's house, a desolate woman' (2 Sam.13:20).

9   2 Samuel 13:22. Absalom decides to ignore Amnon totally. Amnon was older than Absalom and possibly more powerful. If any justice was to be done in the matter, David would need to take the initiative.

10 It is puzzling to consider why no immediate action was taken. Perhaps David was morally compromised and could not afford to punish his own son. The consequences of having lived by his own appetites mean that David is unable to challenge the unrestrained lust of his own son. Absalom prefers to plot his revenge carefully. He knows exactly what he will do to vindicate his sister's honour (2 Sam. 13:32).

[11] 2 Samuel 13:25. Absalom invites David and the whole royal household. David points out that such an entourage would be an impractical burden to his son, but urges him to go ahead with the festival.

[12] David was surprised because Absalom had acted for two years as if Amnon didn't exist (see 2 Sam. 31:22). Why had Absalom changed his mind?

[13] This was a reasonable inference in the circumstances. All of them stood as potential rivals to Absalom.

[14] It is intriguing to consider how Jonadab knew this. Had he been present at the sheep-shearing festival? Or had Absalom taken him into his confidence as a co-conspirator against Amnon?

[15] 2 Samuel 13:34-36. The scene described by the narrator must have been quite a sight in Jerusalem. Loud wailing and weeping on the part of the royal family would have set the city ablaze with rumour.

[16] 2 Samuel 3:2 describes Absalom's mother as 'Maacah daughter of Talmai king of Geshur'. The king of Geshur is now Ammihud (2 Sam. 13:37) who was probably a close relative of Absalom's mother – possibly her brother. Absalom finds sanctuary there for a period of three years.

[17] This is the clear inference of 2 Samuel 13:39. Perhaps he comes to terms with Amnon's death by reasoning that justice had been done. But Absalom's absence seemed more than David could bear: '..the spirit of the king longed to go to Absalom …'

[18] Joab was David's nephew as well as one of his closest confidantes (see 1 Chr. 2:15-16).

[19] 2 Samuel 14:2. She is described as a 'wise woman' which may well suggest that she had some prophetic gifting and was used to help bring God's direction into people's lives. Why Joab chose her above any other woman suggests that he realised David's condition needed divine intervention.

[20] 2 Samuel 14:7.

[21] 2 Samuel 14:8-9. There is a suggestion that David is reluctant to act as he could be seen as condoning murder by pardoning the guilty son. Some suggest he is avoiding the decision and by putting the woman off is hoping that the fugitive will be found and killed. The woman's response that any blood guilt should be upon

her in this matter may be a response to David's dilemma. If he was scared of the responsibility of pardoning a murderer, then she would bear the weight herself.

22   2 Samuel 14:10-11. The woman pushes her case as far as she can. If David was hoping to put her off with a deferred decision he was disappointed. The incident is reminiscent of the parable of the persistent widow (Lk. 18:1-8).

23   2 Samuel 14:14. The woman appeals to the character of God who seeks after those who have wandered from him, offering the chance of forgiveness and a new start. She challenges David to consider why he is unable to follow the standards set by the God he claims to worship.

24   2 Samuel 14:17. Joab's carefully designed plan must not offend David and so the language is carefully chosen to imply respect and honour.

25   2 Samuel 14:19-20. The fact that David quickly identifies Joab behind this 'case' suggests that the two of them had shared conversations concerning Absalom's future. The woman is keen to point out that 'Your servant Joab did this to change the present situation …'

26   2 Samuel 14:24. David's decision was a half-way house. Absalom was allowed back – but life could not go on for him as before. Perhaps David feels his own responsibility for failing to act when Amnon raped Tamar and is now conscious that he needs to act with justice. Absalom is allowed back but he is to be punished by internal exile.

27   2 Samuel 14:27. There is deep significance here. Absalom offered in his daughter Tamar a chance for her aunt perhaps to find some comfort.

28   2 Samuel 14:32. Absalom is taking a calculated risk, for the king could order his execution. But he is hopeful that his three years exile in Geshur followed by two years of virtual house arrest in Jerusalem will be seen as a sufficient punishment for his murder of Amnon.

29   2 Samuel 14:33.

30   2 Samuel 12:10 – the word of the Lord came to David: 'the sword shall never depart from your house, because you despised me and took the wife of Uriah the Hittite to be your own.' David is now witnessing the fulfilment of these words.

[31] Galatians 6:7.

[32] Galatians 5:22-23.

[33] 2 Samuel 13:20.

[34] Isaiah 53:5.

[35] 2 Samuel 3:2-5. David married several women as part of political alliances.

[36] 2 Samuel 12:13. David's repentance met with the pardon of God. By contrast he seemed unwilling or unable to deal with Absalom's sin. The Lord 's Prayer comes to mind: 'Forgive us our sins as we forgive those who sin against us.' Learning to deal with others on the basis of God's dealing with us seems to be a fundamental requirement of the spiritually effective life.

[37] Surveys published in the summer of 2001 indicated that Britain's teenagers cite these two sources as important influences in helping them to make moral choices.

[38] 2 Samuel 13:32.

[39] Ephesians 4:20-32.

[40] Matthew 5:9.

[41] 2 Samuel 14:14. This is a remarkable Old Testament statement about the character of God and foreshadows much of the New Testament teaching on grace.

[42] 2 Samuel 14:1 – 'Joab son of Zeruiah knew that the king's heart longed for Absalom.'

21

Rejected

Listening to the story – 2 Samuel 15:1 – 18:33

David and Absalom may have a surface reconciliation but the cancer in their relationship is advancing fast. Soon Absalom begins a blatant attempt to seize power for himself, laying the foundations for a bloody overthrow of his father's regime.[1] He launches an enormously successful public relations campaign. His plan has three main strands:

The appearance of personal power

By providing himself with a smart chariot and a large squad of security guards, Absalom creates the aura of power around himself.[2]

The promise of a brighter tomorrow

By rising early, Absalom meets people coming to the capital from various parts of the country to place their petitions for justice before the king. He asks to review their case and always endorses their complaint, sympathising that the palace bureaucracy is not delivering justice. He then adds the tanta-lising comment, 'But of course, if I was appointed as judge in such matters then you wouldn't have this log-jam.'[3]

The stroking of people's egos

Absalom cynically treats people as special, offering them particular attention and the sort of greeting reserved only for close friends and family.[4]

In the words of the narrator,[5] 'he stole the hearts of the men of Israel.[6] The stage is set for a violent transfer of power. Eventually, Absalom asks David for permission to go to Hebron and fulfil a vow he made some time previously. David grants permission for what appears to be an innocent request. In fact Absalom is initiating the final stage of his plan. He sends messengers across Israel with a secret message: 'As soon as trumpets are heard across the land then you will know Absalom has been crowned king in Hebron.'

Cleverly, he has invited two hundred influential men from Jerusalem to Hebron as his special guests. They accept in innocence, not realising that they will soon find themselves trapped at the centre of a coup. He also sends for David's most trusted adviser, Ahithophel. The groundswell of support for Absalom is growing and David's hold on power begins to look very shaky.[7] More and more are coming over to Absalom's side. He has built popular support away from Jerusalem so as not to draw attention to his plot. But now the coup can be kept secret no longer.

A messenger brings David devastating news. The message simply says, 'The hearts of the men of Israel are with Absalom.'[8] David immediately plans to leave Jerusalem, the only way to avoid a bloodbath. He leaves ten of his concubines behind to take charge of the palace and to look after its contents.[9] He is accompanied by his household and personal guard which included foreign troops, showing great loyalty. This is epitomised by Ittai who declines David's invitation to go back to his homeland. Ittai's loyalty is echoed by others close to David and this proves vital in his retaining the throne.[10]

David flees from the city with his large entourage. Public emotion and stunned shock greet the royal party as they make their way through the Kidron Valley and out into the surrounding countryside.[11]

Accompanying the party are Zadok the priest, together with the Ark, carried by the Levite priests. David tells Zadok to go back to Jerusalem with the Ark. On the surface this is surprising as the Ark is a powerful symbol of Yahweh's presence with his people. If you possess the Ark then it makes a statement about your 'acceptability' before God. But David reveals his heart when he tells Zadok, 'Take the ark of God back into the city. If I find favour in the Lord's eyes, he will bring me back and let me see it and his dwelling place again. But if he says, "I am not pleased with you," then I am ready; let him do to me whatever seems good to him.'[12]

David points out to Zadok that if he goes back with the Ark, he can pass on vital information about Absalom's plans.[13] David gives similar instructions to another loyal friend – Hushai, to act as a mole in Absalom's new administration. David is alarmed to hear that his chief adviser Ahithophel has chosen to side with Absalom[14] – and he prays that his advice will fail.

David's withdrawal from Jerusalem meets with a mixed response. David, his household and the surrounding populace are sad.[15] Some – like Shimei – curse David to his face.[16] Ziba, a rank opportunist, uses the situation for his own advantage.[17] Both will appear later when David is vindicated and restored to the throne.

Absalom quickly establishes himself in his father's palace in Jerusalem. He must be surprised at such a bloodless takeover – David flees without any show of resistance. Absalom is further surprised to discover Hushai – one of his father's closest advisers – willing to change sides. When he questions this, Hushai flatters Absalom that he is so obviously the choice of the people and the Lord, he is happy to support the new regime.[18] Absalom is astounded. Not only is he in power – he has got his father's two most trusted advisers.

He decides to try them out. First, he asks Ahithophel for advice – a man whose counsel was seen as the voice of God.[19]

Ahithophel puts forward a strategy for immediate action. On the political front, he advises Absalom to sleep with the concubines that David left behind, so blatantly that it will

quickly become public knowledge. This would be the ultimate insult that he could throw in his father's face, signalling
a point of no return. Politically, this is an important move. If
any doubt that Absalom is serious in his attempt to take the
throne, they now realise there is no turning back. The advice
is accepted and a tent is pitched on the palace roof so
Absalom can be seen to be sleeping with these women. Soon
the insult is known throughout Israel.[20]

From a military point of view, Ahithophel's advice is
strong. They should mount a force of twelve thousand soldiers
and attack David immediately when he is at his weakest.
David should be assassinated, keeping other casualties to a
minimum. Such a sudden strike would provoke terror among
David's weary troops, who would probably fall with little
resistance. He concludes his advice: 'The death of the man you
seek will mean the return of all; all the people will be
unharmed.'[21]

Absalom and his close advisers are impressed with
Ahithophel's plan and are inclined to implement it. But first,
Absalom asks Hushai to offer his opinion. Hushai has not for-
gotten David's heartfelt pleas[22] and subtly undermines
Ahithophel's advice:

- David is an experienced fighter
- David and his men are fierce fighters, who will not be a
  pushover as Ahithophel suggests
- All Israel knows his reputation – and will expect him to
  attack Absalom first
- Public opinion would be more likely to believe in David's
  superior strength[23]

Hushai has an alternative plan. Absalom should muster all his
available troops and take personal command of his army. He
should then march out at the head of his force and attack
David wherever he finds him. If he seeks refuge in a city then
they should lay siege and destroy the place.[24]

The hand of God was in the outcome of this consultation.
Absalom accepts Hushai's advice, 'For the Lord had determined

to frustrate the good advice of Ahithophel in order to bring disaster on Absalom.'[25]

Hushai confides all this to Zadok and Abiathar, the priests.
They in turn pass the information to their sons, Jonathan and
Ahimaaz, who escape and get the vital message to David. He
and his entourage flee across the Jordan, grateful that the loyal
Hushai has bought them a few hours of extra time.[26]

Meanwhile Ahithophel is unable to live with the disgrace of
his advice being spurned. Setting his house in order, he hangs
himself.[27]

David has regrouped with his troops in the city of
Mahanaim to the north east of Jerusalem on the far side of the
Jordan River. They receive supplies from the neighbouring
leaders who seem keen to support David in the impending
battle. Absalom sets out at the head of his army under the
command of Amasa.[28]

David reorders his troops into three companies under the
command of Joab, Abishai and Ittai. Although David wants to
go out with the troops, his commanders urge him to stay and
offer support from the comparative safety of Mahanaim,
recognising that David is the chief target in this campaign.[29]
He accepts their advice and sends his troops off to fight the
decisive battle with one important instruction to every commander: 'Be gentle with the young man Absalom for my
sake.'[30]

The site of the battle is the forest of Ephraim, situated north
of the Jabbok River in the Transjordan. David's army is made up
of experienced fighters who rout Absalom's forces, leaving a
massive twenty thousand casualties in a single day of fighting.[31]

Surprised by some of David's men, Absalom tries to escape.
His long hair catches in the branches of an oak tree and his
mule flees, leaving him hanging in mid-air. The pursuing soldiers are afraid to kill the king's son and, instead, bring word
to Joab, their commander. He throws three javelins into
Absalom's dangling body before letting ten of his men
butcher him.[32]

Absalom is buried without much ceremony and the remainder of his troops flee.[33] Ahithophel was right after all.[34]

Arrangements are made for the news to be taken to David, and his world collapses. His victory and the security of his throne are eclipsed by the dreadful news that his son is dead. His grief is obvious to all as he cries, 'O my son Absalom! My son, my son Absalom! If only I had died instead of you – O Absalom, my son, my son!' [35]

Learning from the story

Some suggest that David's Jerusalem years saw his walk with God deteriorate. Being on the run from Saul kept his faith sharp and alive. When peace and prosperity came, the priority of God in his life seemed to slip. [36]

If that is the case then Absalom's rebellion and the tragic aftermath served as a powerful wake-up call for the complacent king.

Three elements from the story speak to us.

- Prodigals
- Pain
- Providence

Prodigals

The Absalom story reminds us (painfully) that family relationships do not all work out well. David's alienation from his son echoes separations that we sometimes share. Hopefully, our prodigal experience will not end in such a tragic way. But we are reminded of several things concerning prodigals:

- They exist
- The fault is not all theirs
- Our attitude to them is more important than their attitude to us
- We need to make the way home easy for them
- Church is (or should be) all about returned prodigals

Pain

When we hurt physically, it is a wonderful relief to hear some-one say, 'Can I give you something to ease the pain?' Sadly, some of us have such severe symptoms, relief is only mar-ginal or temporary. But 'soul pain' is in a different league. When you are living with loss, there is a deep ache that can be felt physically. And there are no pills for that kind of pain.

What did David do?

He recovered his relationship with God. Suffering does one of two things; it either draws us to God or drives us away from God. Two psalms give us a glimpse of David's inner life at this time. Believed to have been written around the height of this crisis, they tell us how David dealt with the pain of betrayal and loss.

Pain and betrayal – Psalm 55

Ahithophel's decision to join Absalom devastates David and he lays bare his heart about this betrayal.[37] In spite of this treacherous act he makes a conscious choice to put his hope in God alone.[38] Here is faith when the chips are down. It is easy to sing when we're winning, but some of God's best tunes are night music.

Pain and loss – Psalm 3

This is a much briefer prayer – but no less real. Deep prayers do not have to be long ones. David knows the outlook is bleak and many people are saying this is the end for him.[39] But for all of that, he is fixing his eyes upon God[40] and is determined to enjoy the sleep of faith[41], believing that his hope is in God alone.[42]

David's experience of pain drew him closer to God. Where does pain drive us?

Providence

David showed a remarkable sense of God's overruling provi-dence as this disaster unfolded. Remember how he sent the

Ark back to Jerusalem rather than rely on some superstitious faith bound up with icons and talismans?[43] Or how he prayed when confronted by Ahithophel's disloyalty?[44] Or how he responded to Shimei's curses, believing that God might be speaking to him through them?[45]

This is not fatalism but faith. David recalled that his time was in God's hands and that when he lived consciously trusting in God's providential care, he was at his best.

I recall visiting the home of a Christian minister. On his living room wall was a large cartoon print. It showed a tug of war between a team of small angels and a team of bigger, tougher looking demons. The characters were straining to beat the opposition and the look on the angels' faces suggested that the demons were winning. But at the end of the angel line, one of the team was half turned and had a confident grin on his face. He could see what the rest of his team couldn't see – a huge hand coming down from the sky, with the thumb firmly planted on the end of the angels' rope.

The message was clear. There was no way they were going to lose.

That is providence.

---

[1] 2 Samuel 15:1. The narrator records that this was 'in the course of time'. The link with the conclusion of the previous chapter seems to be that David's acceptance of Absalom drew a line underneath the murder of Amnon, whereas Absalom had decided to overthrow his father.

[2] 2 Samuel 15:1.

[3] 2 Samuel 15:2-4. These complainants were not getting through to see the king as there was no-one to hear their cases, possibly indicating David's increasing lack of a grip on what was going on. Absalom capitalised on this weakness.

[4] 2 Samuel 15:5-6. Absalom knew how to 'work the room'. He was climbing the slimy power pole. What a contrast to all that God had achieved in appointing and anointing his father David.

[5] According to 2 Samuel 15:7 this went on for four years during which time word about Absalom had spread throughout Israel.

[6] 2 Samuel 15:6.

⁷ 2 Samuel 15:7-12. How could all this happen without David knowing – or at least suspecting – what his son was up to? Did David ignore any warnings? Or was he now so 'out of touch' that Absalom could build a personal power base unchallenged? Either way, it reveals how the legacy of the Bathsheba affair lingered long into David's reign.

⁸ 2 Samuel 15:13.

⁹ 2 Samuel 15:14-18. Why did David flee? He was a wily tactician and realised he stood a better chance of success if he withdrew and regrouped.

¹⁰ 2 Samuel 15:19-21.

¹¹ 2 Samuel 15:23.

¹² 2 Samuel 15:25. This is not so much fatalism on David's part as an expression of faith. Whether or not the Ark was with him would make no difference to the situation. His future was in God's hands.

¹³ 2 Samuel 15:27.

¹⁴ Ahithophel's disloyalty could be explained by the fact that he was Bathsheba's grandfather. He may have felt aggrieved at the way in which David had treated her and damaged his family (see 2 Sam. 11:3, 23:34).

¹⁵ 2 Samuel 15:23, 30.

¹⁶ 2 Samuel 16:5-14. Shimei was from the late King Saul's clan and saw what was happening as judgement on David.

¹⁷ 2 Samuel 16:1-4. Ziba was servant to Mephibosheth, the son of Jonathan whom David had treated with great kindness. He (falsely) tells David that Mephibosheth has decided to side with Absalom.

¹⁸ 2 Samuel 16:16-19.

¹⁹ 2 Samuel 16:23. Both David and Absalom regarded Ahithophel highly.

²⁰ 2 Samuel 16:21-22. Seizing the royal harem was seen as evidence that an individual had truly seized power. Such an insult ruled out any possible reconciliation between David and Absalom.

²¹ 2 Samuel 17:3.

²² 2 Samuel 15:34.

²³ 2 Samuel 17:7-10.

²⁴ 2 Samuel 17:11-13. Hushai's advice is designed to buy David valuable time. It would take some days to muster a large force to fight, meaning David could escape and regroup with his own troops.

25 2 Samuel 17:14.

26 2 Samuel 17:15-22. The escape of Jonathan and Ahimaaz is further evidence of God's intervention in all that is happening.

27 2 Samuel 17:23. This underlines the depth of disgrace felt by Ahithophel.

28 2 Samuel 17:24-29.

29 2 Samuel 18:1-3. David has lost none of his courage, it seems.

30 2 Samuel 18:5.

31 2 Samuel 18:6-7.

32 2 Samuel 18:9-15. The reluctant soldier knew of David's order to his commanders and was afraid to kill Absalom. Joab recognised that Absalom would always pose a threat. He had already acted as a peace broker between father and son and this had only produced an armed rebellion.

33 2 Samuel 18:18 records that the only monument to Absalom was one he erected himself, either before he had any sons or after the death of the three referred to in 2 Samuel 14:27. The reference to this monument is probably made to underline the disgrace of his death as a rebel against his father. A prince would normally have a lavish tomb.

34 2 Samuel 17:3. Ahithophel had declared (prophesied?) that the death of one man would mean that the majority of the people would be unharmed. He was right, only the 'one man' was Absalom – not David.

35 2 Samuel 18:33.

36 See, for example, Petersen, *Leap Over A Wall*, p198ff, where he suggests David's rejection of Absalom is evidence of a heart cold towards God: 'As he became less compassionate with those around him, he became less passionate with the God within him.'

37 Psalm 55:12-14.

38 Psalm 55:22-23.

39 Psalm 3:1-2.

40 Psalm 3:3-4.

41 Psalm 3:5-6.

42 Psalm 3:7-8.

43 2 Samuel 15:25.

44 2 Samuel 15:31.

45 2 Samuel 16:5-14.

22

Mourning

Listening to the story – 2 Samuel 19:1 – 20:26

David's grief spread like a dark cloud across Mahanaim. The victorious army expect a celebratory parade but find themselves at a wake. Instead of marching proudly, the troops slink back into the city as though defeated.

David is in deep shock as he comes to terms with Absalom's death. So great is his grief as a father, he forgets his role as king and leader. Joab – his faithful military commander – does what only a true best friend can do. He speaks the unvarnished and uncomfortable truth that David needs to hear.

Joab tells him that he is humiliating his valiant army who risked their lives for him. His sharp accusation stings David back to reality: 'You love those who hate you and hate those who love you.'[1]

He warns that unless David acts fast, within hours there will not be a man left on his side. He will then face a bigger calamity than he has ever known.

David makes the supreme effort to face the world. Taking his seat in the gateway as a token acknowledgement of the return of his successful army, the broken-hearted king rallies just in time to prevent a fatal haemorrhage of support.[2]

Confusion reigns in the rest of the nation. The people are arguing about what to do next. David has fled the capital and

Absalom who was acclaimed as the new king is now dead. A power vacuum has been created and some are openly questioning the delay in sending for David to retake his throne.[3]

David seizes the initiative by sending a message to Zadok and Abiathar, the priests. He asks them to approach the elders of his home clan of Judah and enquire why they are so slow in welcoming back one of their own.

He includes with his message an invitation to Amasa who had acted as Absalom's commander.[4] The invitation was a subtle plan to extend an olive branch not only to Amasa but to the troops he had commanded on Absalom's behalf. David confirms his appointment as head of the Israeli army thus sidelining Joab.[5]

The men of Judah invite David to return immediately, so the king and his loyal troops return to the Jordan. An eager posse sets out to meet the returning monarch, each with different motives for their visit.

Shimei, who cursed David as he fled from Jerusalem, comes to offer an abject apology. Ziba and his master, Mephibosheth, also arrive. Shimei who fears he will be killed for his audacity instead finds forgiveness.[6] Mephibosheth and Ziba receive similar grace from David – this appears to be a day for handing out favours rather than settling scores.[7]

The narrator then commends a wealthy benefactor who has proved a true friend to David. Barzillai the Gileadite sheltered David in Mahanaim, providing for him at the height of the crisis over Absalom. He accompanies the king to the Jordan River. David urges him to come to Jerusalem, where he can live as an honoured guest. But Barzillai, now eighty, pleads to be allowed to return home for his remaining years. Instead he sends his son Kimham as his personal representative.[8] This may be prompted by the need for increased security around David. He needs people close to him that he can trust.

David discovers a still divided nation across the Jordan. Only half the troops have come out in his support, although the whole of his own clan of Judah are fully behind him. Even among his supporters there is a fierce argument over who deserves praise for bringing the king back. Clearly David faces an uphill task in restoring a divided nation.[9]

This friction gives rise to another attempted rebellion led by an opportunist called Sheba, from Saul's Benjamite tribe, whose rebellion seems to have been sparked by tribal rivalry. David sees within this rebellion an even greater threat than that posed by Absalom. He senses that there is a crisis of confidence within the nation. People are confused and against such a backdrop it would be easy to imagine Sheba's challenge rapidly gaining credibility.[10]

On returning to Jerusalem, David acts quickly, placing the violated concubines in isolation yet ensuring that they are properly provided for.[11] Secondly, he tells his new commander, Amasa, to summon the fighting men of Judah for a meeting and he gives him three days to deliver. For some reason Amasa fails and this creates great tension for David.[12] He immediately orders Abishai (brother of Joab)[13] to rally those troops that had fought with David against Absalom. They move out mobilised for battle. Eventually Amasa joins them and Joab chooses the moment carefully to murder the man who has become a deadly rival. He stabs Amasa to death.[14] Amasa's dying body becomes a macabre rallying point as one of Joab's men calls the troops to follow his master. But the sight of Amasa becomes counter-productive and the body is moved from view.[15]

Sheba and his troops take shelter in a city about twenty-five miles north of the Sea of Galilee. Joab leads the army of those loyal to David and lays siege to the city.[16] As Joab begins to batter the walls, a wise woman makes a deal that saves the city and delivers Sheba into Joab's hands. She makes an impassioned plea on behalf of her fellow residents, citing their value to the nation as a whole.[17]

Joab explains that his sole objective is the death of Sheba because he has rebelled against David. The woman negotiates with the leaders of the city and Sheba is murdered and his head thrown over the walls. Joab stays true to his word, withdraws his troops and returns to Jerusalem.[18]

He has good news for the king – David's throne is secured and, in turn, so is Joab's position as commander of the army. The narrator concludes this turbulent episode with a run-down of the names of those within the revised hierarchy of David's palace in Jerusalem.[19]

When compared with the list given some years earlier, we notice that some have gone and others have stayed. Most poignant of all is the lack of reference to the king's sons who had once been royal advisers.[20] The long-term impact of the Bathsheba affair was colossal. Two of David's sons, Amnon and Absalom, are now dead and he has almost lost the throne in the face of two separate rebellions.

Truly, the wages of sin is death.[21]

Learning from the story

This episode from David's life offers some insights into wise living. In particular four truths stand out:

- An insight into grief
- An insight into truth
- An insight into relationships
- An insight into Jesus

An insight into grief

Grief can have a crippling effect upon an individual and those around them. Grief follows loss – and that can apply to a host of situations. Most often we think of bereavement, but marriage breakdown, redundancy, chronic illness or estrangement can produce deep grief.

David was so devastated by Absalom's death that life could not go on as normal for him. From this we are reminded of two important things. First, that grief is part of our human experience. That is why the comfort of others for those who live with grief is so important. Second, although we never lose it we can learn to live with grief. David had to reach a decision that many of us face – how he was going to live the rest of his life.[22] At such times we – like David – are called to prove the sufficiency of the grace of God.

An insight into truth

Joab was a ruthless man as the way he dealt with Amasa his rival reveals. He killed Absalom, thus inducing David's bitterness towards him. However, he was fiercely loyal to David and conscious of the need to defend the throne. Indeed, it could be argued that his actions towards Amasa and Absalom were the product of his intense desire to protect it.

His role in speaking a tough word into David's life is worthy of close study. God used him to bring a wake-up call to David at a vital moment.[23] His intervention spurred David into action. If David had ignored Joab and stayed locked into his personal grief, he could have lost the throne. As Proverbs says, 'Wounds from a friend can be trusted.'[24]

We should heed such wounds and cultivate friendships where we can both give, and receive, words of truth.

An insight into relationships

Like David we meet people who hate us, people who hurt us and people who help us. His responses to each are not perfect, but they are instructive.

People who hate us

David could have pursued revenge so far as loud-mouthed Shimei was concerned, but instead he chose to forgive.[25] In choosing this way David demonstrates the principle enunciated by his 'greater Son' in the famous Sermon on the Mount: 'You have heard that it was said, "Love your neighbour and hate your enemy." But I tell you: Love your enemies and pray for those who persecute you, that you may be sons of your Father in Heaven.'[26]

People who hurt us

David never discovers what was going on with Mephibosheth and Ziba. He draws a line under it and once again shows a generosity of spirit.[27] We can learn much from this example and turn a new page with people who have hurt us. Like David, we may never get to the truth but we need to decide to move on, looking to the future rather than fretting about the past.

You can't walk far or fast when you are constantly looking over your shoulder.

People who help us

David's generous heart is seen in his kindness to Barzillai, a faithful friend that David did not forget. Even when Barzillai refuses David's offer of hospitality, the offer is extended to his son instead. Learning to express our thanks is important, and recognising those who have helped us is an essential component in developing a gratitude attitude.

An insight into Jesus

There is within this story a powerful picture of the return of the Lord Jesus Christ. It is an allegory that reminds us of the need to be ever watchful.

David's story is about the return of the king. His return brought mixed reactions. Shimei was ashamed and afraid, Mephibosheth was full of excuses – but there were many like Barzillai who were delighted that all they had worked for had come to pass.

We remember that the King is coming, and we need to be watchful and ready.[28] There will be those like Shimei who will be ashamed and afraid. There will be others like Mephibosheth – full of excuses. And there will be those like Barzillai who have longed and looked for the day and will welcome the King with sheer delight.

How do you face that day – with terror or with joy?[29]

David is back on his throne in Jerusalem after the most turbulent period of his reign. God had appointed him as king – but through his own sin he had almost lost the throne. His family was devastated as Nathan's prophecy came to pass.[30]

The Story of David

He had passed through the fire – and for the rest of his life he would smell the smoke and feel the burns.

---

1 2 Samuel 19:6. David was acting in a way that would make an onlooker believe this was how he felt.

2 2 Samuel 19:8. David probably took the lead in some sort of military parade as his successful troops were officially recognised. Joab's intervention was timely, although we should remember that his hands were covered with Absalom's blood (see 2 Sam. 18:14). Were his actions prompted more by guilt than by loyalty?

3 2 Samuel 19:10. The narrator summarises the intense public debate. To some it seemed obvious David must be invited back – but others were paralysed and unable to act, possibly because of fear of reprisals against those who had supported Absalom.

4 2 Samuel 17:25. Absalom had appointed Amasa as commander of the army of Israel in place of Joab, who had stayed loyal to David.

5 As well as creating an amnesty through this decision, David was also indicating his displeasure with Joab as the one who killed his son Absalom.

6 2 Samuel 19:16-23. David is magnanimous in victory.

7 2 Samuel 19:24-30. David questions Mephibosheth about his decision to support Absalom's rebellion. Mephibosheth protests that his servant Ziba had lied and that his intentions had been honourable throughout. David had given Ziba Mephibosheth's property (16:3) but now divides it equally between them. Mephibosheth appears to decline as his only concern is (apparently) David's welfare. Which of these two was telling the truth?

8 1 Kings 2:7. It would appear that one of Barzillai's sons, Kimham, had shown great kindness to David when he faced this crisis. David later urges his son Solomon never to forget their kindness.

9 2 Samuel 19:40-43. The northern tribes were obviously divided over David's return yet claimed a greater share in the king than the people of Judah. It reveals a nation in shock, led by a man in mourning.

10 2 Samuel 20:1-7. Sheba's rallying call attracted the whole of Israel – only Judah stayed steadfastly loyal to David. As a skilful leader

David understood this move would gather momentum unless he acted fast.

[11] 2 Samuel 20:3. Absalom's actions had scandalised Israel. David acts swiftly and honourably. The women are not punished but are isolated. David cannot pretend Absalom had not committed this grossly offensive act. Such is the injustice of a chauvinistic society that these women were doubly abused.

[12] 2 Samuel 20:4-6. Why did Amasa take so long – incompetence or a more sinister reason? For example, did he think his delay would damage David irreparably and speed Sheba's cause?

[13] 1 Samuel 26:6.

[14] 2 Samuel 20:8-10. The narrator makes no comment on the morality of Joab's actions. Joab had been replaced by David but by the end of the chapter is firmly back in charge again (see 2 Sam. 20:23).

[15] 2 Samuel 20:11-13.

[16] 2 Samuel 20:14-15. The text suggests that Joab's army is of greater strength than Sheba's. Why else would Sheba withdraw into a city for protection? Support for Sheba had obviously dwindled.

[17] 2 Samuel 20:18-19. This wise woman refers to the fact that her city is known for its wisdom, peacefulness and faithfulness. Why destroy such a valuable asset that had become 'a mother in Israel'?

[18] 2 Samuel 20:20-22. This victory – achieved without deaths or casualties – did much to re-secure Joab's position. He had removed Sheba, the principal opposition to David, but not at the expense of many lives. The way was clear for David to consolidate the kingdom and bring back stability across the tribes.

[19] 2 Samuel 20:23-26.

[20] 2 Samuel 8:16-18.

[21] Romans 6:23.

[22] A story was told of Queen Elizabeth the Queen Mother at the time of her death in April 2002. A close friend spoke of the comfort she had received from the Queen Mother when her husband had died. She had asked the question, 'Does it get better?' to which the Queen Mother replied, 'No, but you get better at it.'

[23] 2 Samuel 19:1-7.

[24] Proverbs 27:6.

[25] 2 Samuel 19:21-23.

[26] Matthew 5:43-44.

[27] 2 Samuel 19:24-30.

[28] Matthew 24:42-44 – here Jesus lays down the principle that we should always be ready for his return.

[29] Revelation 6:15-17.

[30] 2 Samuel 12:10.

Reflecting

Listening to the story – 2 Samuel 23:1-23, 24:1-25

David's life is drawing to its final stages. His forty-year reign as king is coming to an end and he reflects what has happened during that time.[1] In line with his gifting, David uses lyrics to record his feelings.[2]

His psalm is all about Yahweh, the Lord of heaven and earth. In his song he boasts about all the Lord has done for him;

- Exalted – the Lord chose him and raised him up for a purpose.[3]
- Anointed – he recalls the anointing that took place when Samuel visited his home in Bethlehem, the second anointing that occurred when the men of Judah recognised his God-ordained kingship and then, finally, the anointing that confirmed him as ruler over all Israel. As David charts his sometimes tortuous progress, he realises it is the anointing of God on his life that has marked him out and preserved him.[4]
- Chosen – David acknowledges that the Lord spoke to and through him. He has been used as an instrument of the Lord and has sought to exercise his rule under divine mandate.[5]

● Blessed – David trusts in the mercy and grace of God to cover his past failures and to bring to fruition all he has promised for the future.[6]

Here is the song of a grateful man and an abiding testimony to the kindness of his God.

The narrator records the thirty-seven names of a group referred to as 'David's mighty men',[7] an elite squad who supported David from his days in the cave of Adullam throughout his reign.[8] There is a distinction between two groups in the list, the Three and the Thirty.

The Three were[9]

● Josheb-Basshebeth
● Eleazar
● Shammah

Highlights of their bravery are recorded as examples of their loyal service to David. The Three were led by Abishai, the brother of Joab.[10] He, too, is commended for his courage.

Turning to the Thirty mighty men, an astounding story of audacious bravery is recounted. Three of the Thirty broke through enemy lines to get David a drink from his favourite well.[11] He took this reckless act of bravery as an opportunity to offer the water as a gift of thanksgiving to God.

The Thirty mighty men are named[12] – although more than thirty names are included in the list. This is probably because this élite corps was always kept at the level of thirty and others were added as members died. With a note of deep poignancy, the final name on the list is recorded – Uriah the Hittite.[13]

The second book of Samuel closes with what one writer describes as 'a puzzling chapter for a modern reader'.[14] David takes a census of the nation, without God's instruction and against wise advice.[15] Pride lay at the heart of David's decision and momentary forgetfulness that it was not his own strength that had brought him to kingship.

After the census has been taken,[16] David readily acknowledges his sin before God. The Lord offers him a choice of one of three punishments and he opts for a three day plague. Seventy thousand Israelis die before the plague is halted at the threshing-floor of a man named Araunah.[17] Under the orders of the prophet Gad, David purchases the threshing-floor from Araunah so that an altar can be built there and sacrifices offered to Yahweh. Araunah – deeply honoured by the king's interest – offers the property freely together with the animals for the sacrifice.

David refuses Araunah's generosity with a famous state-ment: 'I will not sacrifice to the Lord my God burnt offerings that cost me nothing.'[18] The sacrifice is offered and the plague stops. The threshing floor of Araunah the Jebusite passes into David's hands.

The significance of this deal is soon revealed as this piece of property becomes the site of the Temple to be constructed by David's son, Solomon. In biblical history the location is deeply significant. This was Mount Moriah where the obedient Abraham was prepared to sacrifice his son Isaac.[19]

This was the place of willing sacrifice.

In the same city of Jerusalem, within a short distance of the Temple, another willing sacrifice would one day be offered when Jesus, God's Son and Anointed One, would willingly lay down his life for the sin of the world.

Learning from the story

These latter years of David's full and eventful life offer some helpful insights into the life of faith.

Three words encapsulate those insights

- Faithfulness
- Frailty
- Friendships

Faithfulness

David's psalm in this chapter is preceded by a longer song.[20] Both are full of God and a note of thanksgiving is the constant underlying drumbeat, pounding with praise. David reflects on his life, totally and utterly captivated by the greatness and goodness of the Lord.[21]

How much of our own spiritual life is stunted and retarded because we are more captivated by ourselves than God?

The prophet Jeremiah brought a word straight from God's lips:

> This is what the Lord says:
> 'Let not the wise man boast of his wisdom
> or the strong man boast of his strength
> or the rich man boast of his riches,
> but let him who boasts boast about this:
> that he understands and knows me,
> that I am the Lord, who exercises kindness,
> justice and righteousness
> on earth,
> for in these I delight,'
> declares the Lord.[22]

Frailty

Once again in David's life, we see our reflection. His pride led to an unhealthy burst of self-confidence and the census led to a plague. When we find ourselves chafing against the routines of spiritual disciplines, we remember that such things are designed constantly to remind us of our frailty. Some words of invitation to the Eucharist or Holy Communion express it well,

> Come to this sacred table, not because you must but because you may;
> Come not to testify that you are righteous, but that you sincerely love our Lord Jesus Christ and desire to be his true disciples;
> Come not because you are strong but because you are weak;
> not because you have any claim on heaven's rewards, but because in your frailty and sin you stand in constant need of heaven's mercy and help.[23]

Standing in constant need of heaven's mercy is the posture for growth.

Friendships

The narrator of the David story is keen to remember those who loyally and courageously stood by David. Their names and some clues about their daring exploits are offered. These were brave men who stood against armed soldiers, whose hands 'froze to the sword',[24] who refused to run away and faced danger with naked courage.

God notices the details. No-one looks the same in his eyes. A list of strange-sounding names may raise a smile with us – but they raise a cheer in heaven. David was surrounded by friends who stood with him. We are called to live our lives in community not in isolation. In our service for God we are called to serve one another, for our loyalty to Christ can be expressed through hidden acts of kindness to others.

Why are these names recorded in the Bible? The answer, partly, is that David wanted them to be. When the records were being written he wanted to remember his friends. And there is much we can learn from that simple gesture of loyalty.

It is said that the older a person gets the sharper their memory becomes. Images of childhood are somehow clearer and names long forgotten return with clarion sound.

When King David reflects he is reminded of God's faithfulness, his own frailty and the value of friendships.

When we reflect, what do we remember?

Perhaps we feel daunted by failure or the things we set out to accomplish that never quite worked out. Or we meet the painful recollection of a broken marriage and friendships that have been severed. It may be that we prefer not to look back at all as too many unhappy memories are stirred up. Or we may reflect on a life that has been blessed with good health, a happy family and material comforts. We may have achieved a position of success within our community and the benefits that come with such recognition.

For most of us looking back, we see a patchwork. There have been good times and not so good times. When we consider all David had faced, his life was a curious mixture of experiences. He had enjoyed all the trappings of power – but he had also lived as a fugitive. He had known the blessings of love, friendship and family ties. He also knew about betrayal, hatred and schism. He had known times of intimacy with God when he thought he would burst with praise. But he also slept with another man's wife and organised a murder to cover his tracks.

Through it all, David looks back and is deeply aware of how good God has been. Whatever our story so far, can we trace the touch of God on our lives as David did?

A true story helps us bring things into focus.

Imagine the shock of reading the paper over breakfast and discovering your own obituary. It happened in 1888 to Alfred Nobel, the Swedish chemist and industrialist. Owing to a mix-up at the newspaper office, they confused Alfred with his brother and ran the wrong obituary. Apart from the shock, he experienced acute embarrassment that ultimately led him to a change of direction in his life.

He was a complex, lonely man, who achieved fame through a mixture of brilliance and business acumen. An explosives expert, he invented a safe and manageable form of nitro-glycerine in 1866 and christened it 'dynamite'. He went on to patent other discoveries in the field of explosives and built an empire of eighty companies in twenty different countries to handle his interests, which made him a wealthy man.

But the mistaken obituary concerned him as, for the first time, he saw how the world would remember him. He developed explosives primarily for use in mining and road construction; the obituary portrayed him as making his fortune from the misfortune of war. He saw himself as others saw him, an industrialist who traded in armaments and made money from human misery.

He changed direction, altering the terms of his will to show a different face to the world. He had high ideals for peace and progress and wanted to demonstrate in a tangible way his concern for humanity.

When Nobel died in 1896, the bulk of his fortune was left to endow annual prizes for those who had made the most significant contribution in one of five areas: physics, chemistry, medicine, literature and peace. Instructions were left as to how the prizes would be awarded each year and to the present day they remain prestigious.

Perhaps the best known is the Nobel Peace Prize which has an illustrious list of recipients. It is strange that Nobel's name today is most strongly associated with peace when the false obituary linked him with war. His decision paid off and left the world with a better and happier memory of him.

Alfred Nobel was fifty-five when he read his premature obituary and he lived another eight years. It is never impossible or too late to change direction.

Perhaps as we reflect on our lives, we have a longing to change the script and write a different ending. We can, and there's even a special word for it.

It's called conversion.

---

[1] 1 Chronicles 29:26-28.

[2] 2 Samuel 23:1. These are described as 'the last words of David' suggesting not that they were spoken in his dying moments, but rather were a final psalm of gratitude during the concluding part of his reign.

[3] 2 Samuel 23:1.

[4] 2 Samuel 23:1. David lived under the conscious sense that he was anointed by God. The three anointings are recorded at 1 Samuel 16:1-13; 2 Samuel 2:4 and 5:3.

[5] 2 Samuel 23:2-3. David is aware that God spoke to him with clear instructions about how to rule with righteousness and the fear of God. He is also aware that God has spoken through him – perhaps in the wisdom of his decisions as well as in the inspired prayer-songs he composed.

[6] 2 Samuel 23:5. David claims that his house is 'right with God' which may be a reference to his sin over the Bathsheba affair having been confessed and dealt with.

[7] 2 Samuel 23:8.

⁸ According to 1 Chronicles 11:10 these men were – under God – responsible for the strength of his reign.

⁹ 2 Samuel 23:8-12.

¹⁰ 2 Samuel 23:18 – the NIV refers to him as 'chief of the Three' but there are manuscripts that suggest he was chief of the Thirty.

¹¹ 2 Samuel 23:13-17.

¹² 2 Samuel 23:20-39.

¹³ 2 Samuel 23:39.

¹⁴ *New Bible Commentary*, p332.

¹⁵ 2 Samuel 24:3. Joab (David's most senior commander) challenges his orders and strongly urges the king not to take the census. But David refuses to listen.

¹⁶ 2 Samuel 24:9. It took nine months of hard work to discover there were 1.1 million men available to fight in the event of war.

¹⁷ 2 Samuel 24:1-25. The story of David's census raises a number of difficulties, not least the assertion in v1 that God incited David to this course of action because 'the anger of the LORD burned against Israel'. No mention is made of what led up to this. Perhaps the major reason the incident is recorded is to explain why Solomon chose to build the Temple in this location. It was a place where righteous judgement and mercy met together, providing a foreshadowing of a greater occasion where heaven's love and justice would meet and kiss (see Mt. 27:50-54).

¹⁸ 2 Samuel 24:24. The statement has often been used to point out the importance of sacrificial giving. If what we give hasn't cost much, then where is the important element of sacrifice?

¹⁹ Genesis 22:2.

²⁰ 2 Samuel 22:1-51 which is almost identical to Psalm 18.

²¹ Petersen points out David's use of metaphor in describing God. He is a 'God-noticer', drawing God into every part of life. He adds this: 'In long retrospect over the Jewish and Christian centuries, it's no exaggeration to say that anything we know about God that's not prayed soon turns bad. The name of God without prayer to God is the stuff of blasphemy. The truth about God without love for God quickly becomes oppression. So-called theologians, whether amateur or professional, who don't pray are in league with the devil. Indeed, the devil can be defined as that

species of theologian who knows everything about God but will have nothing to do with him.' Petersen, *Leap Over A Wall*, p207.

[22] Jeremiah 9:23-24.

[23] *Patterns and Prayers for Christian Worship – A Guidebook for Worship Leaders* (Oxford: Oxford University Press, 1991) p81.

[24] 2 Samuel 23:10.

Bequeathing

Listening to the story – 1 Chronicles 28:1-21

Time is running out for David as he makes preparations for his son, Solomon, to succeed him as king of Israel.[1] He calls together a large group of leaders in the nation for a summit meeting.[2] There is just one item on the agenda – David's delayed dream.

He longs to build a permanent resting place for the Ark of the Covenant that is still housed in a tent in the capital city of Jerusalem. Although his dream has been endorsed, David knows the Lord has not chosen him to see the project through. This was to be a task for his son, Solomon.[3]

David tells the gathering of his plans and how God has said he will not see them realised.[4] God has chosen Solomon and David publicly acknowledges this. With great solemnity, David charges his son with the duties of king-ship, urging him to be single-minded in his devotion to the Lord.

> 'And you, my son Solomon, acknowledge the God of your father, and serve him with wholehearted devotion and with a willing mind, for the Lord searches every heart and understands every motive behind the thoughts. If you seek him, he will be found by you; but if you forsake him, he will reject you for ever. Consider

now, for the Lord has chosen you to build a temple as a sanctuary. Be strong and do the work.'[5]

With such a public commissioning, it will be hard for Solomon to ignore his father's final wishes.

David also passes on sets of plans that he has made during the preceding years. He has drawn up plans and made practical arrangements to cover the Temple's operations. David believes these are more than helpful suggestions or bright ideas. The narrator records these are the result of David receiving directions from the Lord. '[David] gave [Solomon] the plans of all that the Spirit had put in his mind ...'[6] 'All this,' David said, 'I have in writing from the hand of the Lord upon me and he gave me understanding in all the details of the plan.'[7]

Through his skill in composing prayer-songs, David knows what it is to be inspired by the Spirit of God. There were times when he burst with a powerful sense of the Lord's presence as he composed a psalm. Words and music tumbled out of him in a torrential outpouring. David knows what it is to be God-driven and God-directed. According to his own words, the plans for the Temple came to him in the same fashion. God inspired the organisation of the drawings and the details. Included in these were

- Plans for the buildings
- The working arrangements for priests and Levites
- The weight of the gold and silver to be used in making the various tools for the Temple ceremonies[8]

David concludes by pointing out the skills available for Solomon to use, urging him to be strong and courageous as he sets about the task.[9]

The king turns his attention from Solomon to his assembled guests and bluntly acknowledges that Solomon is young and has much to learn.[10] David reminds them that the overall objective is to build something for God, not for man.[11] He also pledges his own funds to make the project happen and – having given sacrificially to date – David now adds even more.[12] He asks who among these distinguished leaders is willing to follow suit.[13] David is not disappointed as the leaders respond with willing generosity, as the nation notices.[14]

In this wonderful atmosphere of liberality and partnership David leads his leadership team in an act of worship to the Lord. The words of this prayer have been preserved through the generations.[15]

God is the theme of the prayer as David acknowledges

- The greatness, power and glory of the Lord as ruler of all[16]
- That even the material things that the people have brought ultimately come from the hand of the Lord[17]
- That all humankind are foreigners to God's greatness and our fleeting lives pass swiftly[18]
- The Lord who knows all motives will see that the gifts are brought with transparency of heart and are rooted in love for God[19]
- That his generation were part of the unfolding story of God's covenant love[20]

David pleads that the nation will stay loyal and Solomon will remain devoted, so that the Temple dream can be fulfilled.[21] This glorious God-filled prayer ends with a call to offer praise to Yahweh and the people respond in both words and actions.[22] This was a holy end to a summit meeting.

The following day the worship continues with sacrifices and feasting in the presence of the Lord. This culminated in Solomon's coronation, as David moves off the throne, allowing his son to take his place. The leaders and Solomon's brothers pledge their loyalty to the new monarch and a peaceful succession is achieved.[23]

The narrator ends his account of David's reign with a final summary, recording that he had been king for forty years and 'died at a good old age, having enjoyed long life, wealth and honour'.[24]

David had fulfilled what God had given him to do. After all, he was a man after God's own heart.[25]

Learning from the story

This final episode in David's life could be subtitled 'passing on the torch'; like the Olympic flame-bearers, David has run his leg of the race and now passes the responsibility of kingship to his son, Solomon.

The story contains several truths that remind each succeeding generation of the legacy of hand-over. We receive from those who have gone before us and, in turn, we pass responsibility to those who follow on. As we look at David's actions we are reminded of some important elements in this process.

- Planning
- Praying
- Passing

Planning

An outstanding feature of David's life is his ability to overcome personal disappointment. We cannot begin to understand the depth of personal loss he felt when he received God's words of refusal. Kings normally get what they want and their power is measured by the ability to achieve what others can only dream of. But David in vulnerability expresses not his strength, but his weakness. God said, 'No', is the essence of his message.[26]

David had not lost his dream and made careful preparations so Solomon could turn the dream into reality. He passed on the plans that God had laid within him over the years and months – even down to the finest details, nothing was left out.[27] It would have been easy for David to have made the turning down of his plan into a personal issue. He could have wasted his final years in the barrenness of a spiritual sulk. But this man after God's heart was made of richer, stronger stuff. If he couldn't build, he would make sure his son had everything he needed to get the job done.

There is an earthy, spiritual pragmatism in David's example that challenges us to look at the bigger picture and not settle for simply fulfilling our own petty ambitions. We are faced with some important principles here.

Submit your plans to God

Unless our dreams are given over to God, they can easily become nightmares. David had learned the difference between a good idea and a God idea. We can discover the same when we offer him our plans. People have made a mess of their lives and those of others by wrapping their own selfish plans in spiritual language and railroading everything and everyone to conform.

Need doesn't constitute a call

We are surrounded by many needs and worthy causes. Some of us live with such a heightened sense of responsibility, we believe that we possess the solution to everything. Committed Christians are particularly prone to this attitude and it is neither godly nor sensible. Just because you spot a need does not mean you are the one to meet it. Need doesn't constitute a call. There were sick people on earth when Jesus went around healing; not all received his transforming touch. He lived and worked under the Father's direction, always seeking to 'do the work of him who sent me'[28] and steadfastly refusing to live under the pressure of anyone else's timetable.[29]

Being a custodian of the vision

We can become so wrapped up in a vision that we believe that it cannot be achieved without us. Such a view is based on pride. No-one is indispensable; David reminds us of that. The vision for the Temple was bigger than one man's dreams. Indeed, we have already seen that God had an even bigger project in view that would extend far beyond a religious building. An eternal Kingdom made up of a temple built with living stones was the ultimate objective – and still is.[30] But we, like David, have a part to play in God's plan. And learning to be custodians rather than controllers is the wisest way to serve the vision.

Praying

There is something intensely moving about David's prayer and the solemn context of worship in which it is offered.[31] The building of the Temple involved builders, bricks, noise, dust, scaffold poles, drawings and designs. But it began in the atmosphere of worship. Praise, prayers and sacrifices were offered from people overwhelmed by the goodness of their God. If it was to become a house of prayer then it made sense that it began in prayer.

We should never underestimate the power of prayer. It contains a dynamic that is truly awesome. David had learned to develop an intimacy with God that we have seen reflected in his psalms. He had refused to confine prayer to the formal or religious parts of his life. David worshipped not because he was the monarch and it was expected of him on such occasions. He worshipped because he was a worshipper.

Never minimise prayer to the extent of saying, 'I am afraid I can't do much – I can only pray.' If only we had more who did nothing else but pray! The work of the Kingdom would increase with greater impetus if more of God's people prayed.

In the first church where I served was an elderly saint by the name of Herbert Cann. He was confined to his home and completely blind. His movements were limited and, to outside eyes, there was little observable quality of life. I relished visiting Herbert in his home. In fact I used to save my visits for days when I was feeling low in spirit, because I knew that there would be a touch of heaven in store.

Herbert lived close to God and his life had been touched by revival. He was a man who knew God and – despite his physical limitations – had never forgotten how to pray. I sometimes knelt by the side of this frail old man and asked him to lay his hands on me and pray for the anointing needed to serve well.

I never left disappointed. I thank God that, through the years, others have prayed – and continue to pray – for the work I am seeking to do. I think I know a little of how Solomon felt when he heard his dad pray for him to be faithful and strong in the task ahead.

Passing

It must have been a memorable occasion when David got off the throne and made way for Solomon to take the seat of power.[32] Doubtless David had in mind the need for a smooth transition, but it took humility of a special kind to relinquish the reins.

Such an attitude was mirrored by John the Baptist. This great forerunner of Christ was given a call with two clear instructions; to prepare the way for the Lord and then to get out of the way of the Lord. When asked by those closest to him why Jesus was gaining popularity at the expense of his own, John famously replied, 'He must become greater; I must become less.'[33]

At the right moment David was willing and able to pass on the torch to Solomon. We face the same choice. For some of us who lead, we must be willing for others to take that responsibility forward. Some hold key positions and we need to train others to take over from us. We need to invest energy, time, friendship and support in a new generation. Let them learn from our mistakes, share in our successes and benefit from our confidence.

There is a wonderful statement about David which comes in a sermon preached by the Christian leader, Paul. Contrasting the great king with the greater King, Jesus, Paul pointed out that a day came when David died and was buried. In contrast Jesus died but was raised to life again by God through the power of the resurrection. Paul says this about David: 'For when David had served God's purpose in his own generation, he fell asleep; he was buried with his fathers and his body decayed.'[34]

It is the words, 'when David had served God's purpose in his own generation' that speak so eloquently. He had achieved what God had called him to do. It was not a life of perfection, free from sin or mistakes. But through the changing seasons David had proved God and found his way forward. And Scripture records that he had run well and served the purpose of God in his generation.

The call to us is to do the same.

To aim, in our generation, to be men and women after God's own heart.[35]

---

[1] 1 Chronicles 23:1 notes David's decision that Solomon should succeed him as king. This was based on a direct word from God (1 Chr. 22:7-10). This was a wonderful act of grace on God's part as Solomon was the son born to David from his marriage to Bathsheba (2 Sam. 12:24-25).

[2] 1 Chronicles 28:1. David wanted his plans to be clear so there would be no confusion after his death.

[3] 2 Samuel 7:1-29. **Chapter 17 – Refused** details the circumstances surrounding this decision.

[4] 1 Chronicles 28:3. This account goes further than that in 2 Samuel, offering the explanation why David is not to build the Temple: 'You are not to build a house for my Name, because you are a warrior and have shed blood.'

[5] 1 Chronicles 28:9-10.

[6] 1 Chronicles 28:12.

[7] 1 Chronicles 28:19.

[8] 1 Chronicles 28:12-18.

[9] 1 Chronicles 28:20-21.

[10] 1 Chronicles 29:1. Such a blunt admission may seem lacking in tact (particularly as Solomon was standing there!) but appears to be a calculated move on David's part. He is appealing for their loyalty and help and this culminates in a public appeal for people to sign up their support (see v5).

[11] 1 Chronicles 29:1. This important statement lies at the heart of David's appeal for help.

[12] 1 Chronicles 29:2-5. David appears to have been extravagant in his financial commitment to the project.

[13] 1 Chronicles 29:5. David's approach is instructive. His appeal is based on a clear statement of the vision and a personal commitment to its fulfilment.

[14] 1 Chronicles 29:6, 9. This willing response epitomises what Paul meant when he spoke about cheerful giving in 2 Corinthians 9:7.

[15] 1 Chronicles 29:10-20.

[16] 1 Chronicles 29:10-13.

[17] 1 Chronicles 29:14, 16.

[18] 1 Chronicles 29:15. The humility of David's prayer is underlined when we recall this was an occasion when he was surrounded by all the trappings of royalty. This self-abasement for a commoner is one thing – for a monarch before his senior leaders it is quite another!

[19] 1 Chronicles 29:17.

[20] 1 Chronicles 29:18. David refers to Abraham, Isaac and Jacob (Israel) recalling that his generation is a living fulfilment of God's promise to bless a man and then a family, and through them a nation, and through them the whole world. Genesis 12:1-3 gives the start of this fascinating genealogy of grace.

[21] 1 Chronicles 29:18-19.

[22] 1 Chronicles 29:20. David calls for the leaders to offer their praise to God and they respond with words, but also fall prostrate on the floor.

[23] 1 Chronicles 29:21-25. David's motive was to accomplish a smooth succession and preserve the nation from the sort of civil war that had been sparked by Absalom. David knew that his many sons would vie for power and it could prove a bloody, costly and lengthy process. David was attempting to preserve the nation from bloodshed and give Solomon the best possible start he could have. The Temple could only be built if the nation enjoyed peace and stability. As events turned out, Solomon was challenged over the right to rule by his half-brother Adonijah. But the attempt failed (1 Kgs. 1:1ff).

[24] 1 Chronicles 29:28.

[25] Acts 13:22: Paul is preaching in a synagogue in Pisidian Antioch and refers to David as the man who accomplished what God planned for him to do.

[26] 1 Chronicles 28:2-3. It must have been a humbling experience for David to make this public admission before the most powerful people in the nation.

[27] 1 Chronicles 28:11ff – notice how the weight of items was spelt out (v14), the rotas for those serving in the Temple were explained

(v13) and even how store cupboards were to be used (v11). This plan covered everything.

28 John 9:4.

29 An insight into this is given when Jesus' own family (who at that time did not believe in him) mockingly urged him to adopt a higher profile. He replies, 'The right time for me has not yet come; for you any time is right' (Jn. 7:6).

30 2 Samuel 7:11ff; 1 Peter 2:4-10.

31 1 Chronicles 29:10-22.

32 1 Chronicles 29:23.

33 John 3:30.

34 Acts 13:36.

35 Acts 13:22 where Paul alludes to the record of 1 Samuel 13:14 – 'the Lord has sought out a man after his own heart'.

Postscript

This book was in the final stages of writing when I received an anonymous letter. It was in response to a newspaper article where I had written about the choices we make and the way in which they can affect our lives for good or bad. The particular point I was making was about the choice to forgive, draw a line under the past and move on.

Someone didn't like what I had to say and so, under the cloak of anonymity, thrust a piece of paper through my letter box. The brief note told me to look up some verses in the Bible. What the writer could not have known is that I was thinking about those very verses, because they detail the final days of David's life.

In what may well have been his final conversation with his son, Solomon, David appears less than gracious.[1] Having solemnly charged his son to walk in God's ways, David, surprisingly, encourages him not to forget some old scores and eventually to settle them.[2]

What my anonymous correspondent was pointing out to me was (I think) that even David, the man after God's heart, sought vengeance against those who had wronged him. So – in the cold light of day – forgiveness seems a lofty and worthy ideal, but not one that is attainable. As C.S. Lewis pointed out, everyone thinks forgiveness a wonderful idea, until they have something to forgive.

So what are we to make of this less than gracious, final glimpse of David? There are two important factors to bear in mind before we leap to a hasty and, perhaps, unjust conclusion.

First, as the record shows, David was *fallible*. He made some wrong calls in his life and this may be another. For instance, his desire for revenge almost led him to kill Nabal, and only the timely, gracious intervention of Abigail stopped him.[3] The Bible paints a true picture of David, and this final episode may convey a reminder of his fallibility – and warning about our own.

Secondly, we are told that towards the end of his life, David became increasingly *frail*. There is a rather touching story told of David's poor circulation and his inability to keep warm at night.[4] Someone came up with the bright idea that a beautiful young woman should be found to lie in bed alongside him and provide the warmth he lacked. So Abishag, a Shunamite, enters the palace as a personal aide to the aged king. But the narrator is anxious to point out that this was not a sexual relationship.[5] David was around seventy when he died[6] and this passage suggests his health was breaking down. It is possible, therefore, that some form of dementia was affecting his behaviour and his final instructions to Solomon were influenced accordingly. We understand more today about the ageing process and perhaps this may partly explain David's actions.

Whether or not his desire for revenge was caused by his fallibility or frailty – or a mixture of both – we cannot tell. The unequivocal words of David's greater son, the Lord Jesus Christ, remain clear on forgiveness: 'For if you forgive men when they sin against you, your Heavenly Father will also forgive you. But if you do not forgive men their sins, your Father will not forgive your sins.'[7]

In our own lives, the standard laid down by Christ himself is the one by which our actions must be measured. David's life – as we have seen – comes complete with wrinkles. But his life stands as an eloquent testimony that crumpled people are not beyond usefulness in the hands of God. We who know what it is to be utterly captivated by the high and holy also know how to be brought crashing down by the wicked and the wasteful. Yet David's story reminds us that God shows up in the lives of his flawed people.

I am intrigued by the references in Scripture to the state of David's heart, for it is this which seems to have drawn the Lord to use him so significantly. The man after God's heart offers us an abiding model of how to live well for Christ. It is not a case of ignoring our failures or hiding behind excuses. David's chequered path encourages us to be real. By acknowledging we get it wrong we are encouraged to work harder at getting it right. Discipleship is about journeying.

I want to conclude with a tale of two seas. They offer a parable for those who hunger for a true spirituality and a more meaningful pathway of discipleship.

The Dead Sea is the lowest body of water on planet earth, lying a quarter of a mile below sea level. Sandwiched between Israel and Jordan, it is utterly lifeless. Water flows into the Dead Sea from the Jordan River – but it has no outlet. It is only kept from bursting its banks due to the intense heat of the desert sun which causes the water to evaporate at roughly the same rate as its inflow.

But such a strange phenomenon carries implications. The evaporating water leaves behind salt and other minerals which accumulate to toxic levels that mean no plant or fish life can be supported. Nothing lives in the Dead Sea – and if fish are carried in from the Jordan River, they cannot survive in this place of death.

The Aral Sea is fed by rivers in Kazakhstan and Uzbekistan. In recent years, these rivers have been diverted to support new irrigation developments and the Aral Sea has suffered as a result. It has shrunk by 50 per cent – in one year alone it lost 3,885 square kilometres. Settlements built on the shoreline now find themselves dozens of miles from the sea. The water that is left is badly polluted by pesticides and, as a result, fish stocks have dropped – leading to the collapse of the fishing industry. Scientists charting the process estimate that, within a decade, the Aral Sea could totally disappear.

The Dead Sea is dead because it doesn't flow anywhere. The Aral Sea is dying because less is flowing in. This tale of two seas reminds us that inflow and outflow are essential for life.

The same is true in the spiritual life. We can be inflow people; attending conferences and meetings, collecting tapes and books, busying ourselves at every turn for the next opportunity of finding some personal blessing. But where does it flow? If there is no practical outworking of what I am taking in, then spiritual stagnation beckons. We live in a spectator age when people would rather view than do. The New Testament knows nothing of such things. 'Servanthood', 'discipleship' and 'seeking first the Kingdom of God' are words that all point to lives with a healthy outflow.

Equally, we face the danger of being outflow people. We can be so busy doing, serving, giving, planning and organising that we are in danger of drying up completely. We need to learn the balance of taking in and giving out. David's story reminds us of the importance of an inner life of prayer and worship. The warrior king found time to pray and left us his prayer songs as marker posts. He encourages us to learn how work and worship live best together.

David discovered the balance, as Scripture records:

> He chose David his servant and took him from the sheep pens;
> from tending the sheep he brought him to be the shepherd of his
>   people Jacob,
> of Israel his inheritance.
> And David shepherded them with integrity of heart;
> with skilful hands he led them.[8]

Integrity of heart and skilful hands suggest a balance of the inner and outer life; between what we take in and what we give out; about our life before God in the secret place and our life before the world in the public place.

As we have noted, Paul, the fearless leader of the Church and preacher of Christ, spoke of David serving God's purpose 'in his own generation'.[9] One man who served God well in his generation, citing another, who did the same in his.

Our story is still being written. Will it show that we served Jesus well in our generation and sought, by the power of his Spirit, to live as men and women after God's own heart?

---

[1] 1 Kings 2:1-12

[2] David singles out Joab and Shimei particularly for Solomon to deal with. He is to reward Barzillai's family.

[3] 1 Samuel 25:2ff has the story.

[4] See 1 Kings 1:1-3

[5] See 1 Kings 1:4

[6] 2 Samuel 5:4

[7] Matthew 6:14-15. This statement comes immediately after Jesus had given his disciples 'The Lord's Prayer'. Forgiving and being forgiven are inextricably linked in the prayer and Jesus further underlines the connection between the two with this statement.

[8] Psalm 78:72

[9] Acts 13:36